100 essay plans for economics

Ernie Jowsey

OXFORD

UNIVERSITY PRESS

OXFORD

UNIVERSITY PRESS

Great Clarendon Street, Oxford OX2 6DP

Oxford University Press is a department of the University of Oxford.
It furthers the University's objective of excellence in research, scholarship,
and education by publishing worldwide in

Oxford New York

Auckland   Cape Town Dar es Salaam Hong Kong Karachi
Kuala Lumpur Madrid Melbourne Mexico City Nairobi
New Delhi Shanghai Taipei Toronto
With offices in
Argentina Austria Brazil Chile Czech Republic France Greece
Guatemala Hungary Italy Japan South Korea Poland Portugal
Singapore Switzerland Thailand Turkey Ukraine Vietnam

Oxford is a registered trade mark of Oxford University Press
in the UK and in certain other countries

Published in the United States
by Oxford University Press Inc., New York

ISBN 978-0-19-877592-8

Printed in the United Kingdom by
Lightning Source UK Ltd., Milton Keynes

Contents

List of figures xii

Introduction 1

Microeconomics

Introductory Microeconomics

Plan 1 'Economic theory has no practical value.' Discuss. 11

2 Explain how the concept of opportunity cost measures the real cost of resource allocation decisions. 13

3 Outline the essential differences between free-market and centrally planned economies. Discuss the economic problems which may arise in the transition of the Eastern European economies to the market system. 15

4 Discuss the role of the price mechanism in the allocation of economic resources. 17

5 Compare and contrast the principal economic characteristics of a free-market economy with those of a planned economy. 19

Demand and supply analysis

Plan 6 Why might government intervention, in the form of price ceilings and floors, have undesirable consequences? 23

7 'Price controls are an inefficient method of helping poor people because they always lead to shortages.' Discuss. 25

8 With reference to examples, explain the use that economists make of the concepts of price elasticity of demand and income elasticity of demand. 27

9 Examine the main influences on the price of motor cars. 29

10 Examine the significance of price elasticity of demand in decisions relating to an increase in the tax on tobacco. 31

Markets

Plan 11 Critically discuss the view that advertising promotes market imperfection and is against the interests of consumers. 35

12 Why do manufactured goods typically exhibit greater price stability than is the case with primary products? 37

13 Examine the factors which could be expected to determine the price of houses in a free market. **39**

14 Explain what is meant by the terms 'normal profit' and 'super-normal' or 'abnormal profit'. **41**

15 Explain the reasons for and the effects of government or European Union support for agriculture. **43**

16 Discuss the view that minimum wage legislation will lead to increased unemployment. **45**

17 Explain why it is sometimes argued that taxes should be imposed upon economic rents. **47**

18 Discuss the view that company profit is an unnecessary surplus which should be removed by the imposition of high taxes. **49**

19 Assess the validity of the marginal productivity theory of wages in explaining wage levels in the United Kingdom. **51**

20 Evaluate the success of equal pay legislation in raising women's wages. **53**

Production and costs

Plan 21 Evaluate the extent to which the disadvantages of division of labour outweigh the advantages. **57**

22 Explain, with reference to examples, why small firms continue to exist despite economies of scale. **59**

23 Explain the circumstances under which a firm would continue to produce at a loss. **61**

24 Why do firms seek to grow larger, and are large firms in the public interest? **63**

Firms

Plan 25 What are the main features and predictions of perfect competition? **67**

26 'Firms maximize profits where $MC = AC$.' Discuss. **69**

27 Discuss what you consider to be the most important limits on the size of firms in the long run. **71**

28 What are the main features and predictions of imperfect competition? **73**

29 'The critical assumption of the theory of the firm is barriers to entry.' Discuss. **75**

30 Why is the behaviour of firms in oligopoly difficult to predict? **77**

31 What are the sources of monopoly, and what is the economic case for and against patents? 79

32 Analyse the role of the trade unions in the UK as a monopoly power. 81

33 Compare and contrast alternative methods of dealing with monopoly. 83

34 How is it that sometimes two different prices can be charged for the same product or service? 85

35 Discuss the economic case in favour of monopoly. 87

36 'Cartels are beneficial because they reduce uncertainty.' Discuss. 89

Market efficiency and failure

Plan 37 Explain the distinction between private and social costs and the problems that can result when they diverge. 93

38 Explain how a cost–benefit analysis could be done with reference to an actual or hypothetical project. 95

39 Discuss the arguments for and against cost–benefit analysis. 97

40 Explain how the absence of property rights can lead to market failure. 99

41 Explain why there are inequalities in the present distribution of income and wealth in the United Kingdom. 101

Microeconomic policy

Plan 42 Outline the various supply-side policies which have been introduced in the UK and assess the extent to which they have influenced the performance of the economy. 105

43 Explain the advantages and disadvantages of the privatization of industries such as gas, water, and telecommunications. 107

44 What accounts for the growth in the numbers of self-employed workers in the UK since 1980? 109

45 Discuss the case for and against 'road pricing' in order to reduce traffic congestion. 111

46 How do merit goods differ from private goods? Do these differences affect the way in which they are provided? 113

47 Is there an economic 'North–South Divide' in the UK? 115

48 How is competition encouraged and monopoly discouraged in the UK? 117

49 How has the retail sector of the UK economy changed since 1960? **119**

50 To what extent has the policy of privatization of parts of the UK public sector achieved its objectives since 1979? **121**

Macroeconomics

Introductory Macroeconomics

Plan 51 Show how aggregate demand and aggregate supply can be used to illustrate and explain the level of economic activity and the price level. **127**

52 Explain what is meant by 'value added' and show how it is used in calculating the national product. **129**

53 Explain the concept of 'equilibrium national income'. **131**

54 'Gross national product (GNP) is the best indicator of a country's standard of living.' Discuss. **133**

Consumption

Plan 55 What are the most important determinants of consumer spending? **137**

56 How can the relationship between consumption and income influence government policy? **139**

57 Explain the difference between consumption and investment and discuss in which category you would place education and housing. **141**

Saving

Plan 58 What are the most important determinants of saving? **145**

59 Does the 'paradox of thrift' mean that saving is bad for the economy? **147**

60 Examine the role of interest in determining saving and investment. **149**

Investment

Plan 61 What are the most important determinants of investment? **153**

62 Show how consumer expenditure and investment expenditure influence the level of national income. **155**

63 Are savings and investment always equal? **157**

National income determination

Plan 64 Explain what is meant by the 'balanced budget multiplier'. **161**

65 To what extent can the interaction of the multiplier and the accelerator explain the business cycle? **163**

66 Distinguish between the national income multiplier and the accelerator and discuss their significance for a government's macroeconomic policy. **165**

67 Evaluate the various explanations that have been put forward to explain fluctuations in the level of economic activity. **167**

68 What policies would you advocate to eliminate (1) an inflationary gap and (2) a deflationary gap? **169**

69 Explain how the government can influence the level of interest rates in the economy. **171**

Money and banking

Plan 70 What problems are involved in measuring the supply of money in the UK? **175**

71 Explain how and why monetary policy has changed in the UK since 1979. **177**

72 Explain the main functions of the Bank of England and discuss the role of the Bank of England in controlling inflation. **179**

73 Explain how the money supply is controlled by the monetary authorities in the UK. **181**

74 Why do people keep money in cash and current accounts when in other forms it can earn more interest? **183**

75 Distinguish the money market from the capital market and evaluate the role of the capital market in the UK economy. **185**

Public finance

Plan 76 Discuss how a change in the marginal rate of direct taxation might affect the level of national income. **189**

77 What is the Public Sector Borrowing Requirement (PSBR)? Explain how the PSBR relates to the supply of money in the United Kingdom. **191**

78 How might the government use fiscal policy to influence the economy? **193**

79 Discuss the view that the government ought to aim to balance its budget. **195**

Inflation

Plan 80 Examine the difficulties which can arise in trying to measure the cost of living. **199**

81 Discuss the proposition that inflation is the single most important economic problem. **201**

82 Why have UK governments found it difficult to control inflation? **203**

83 Assess the significance of the Natural Rate of Unemployment Hypothesis for the conduct of economic policy. **205**

84 Discuss how the government's commitment to stable prices is likely to affect the level of unemployment. **207**

Unemployment

Plan 85 Evaluate different economic explanations of the current level of unemployment in the United Kingdom. **211**

86 What are the various factors which determine the level of aggregate output and employment? **213**

87 Discuss whether or not it is possible to reduce unemployment without increasing inflation. **215**

88 Evaluate the economic costs which result from unemployment in the UK. **217**

89 What is meant by the term 'mobility of labour'? Would increasing the mobility of labour reduce unemployment, and if so, how? **219**

International trade

Plan 90 What are the advantages of international trade? Are there any disadvantages? **223**

91 Discuss the likely consequences of a fall in the exchange rate for the balance of payments and the rate of inflation. **225**

92 Explain what is meant by 'the terms of trade'. What might cause these to move in a country's favour? **227**

93 Discuss whether or not the formation of trading blocs such as the European Community contributes to an increase in economic welfare. **229**

Exchange rates

Plan 94 Taking into account recent experience, critically assess the view that 'allowing the pound to float' is better for the United Kingdom than a fixed exchange rate. **233**

95 How does membership of the Exchange Rate Mechanism of the European Monetary System affect a government's ability to pursue an independent monetary policy? **235**

Economic growth

Plan 96 Examine the policies which a government might employ if it wishes to raise the rate of economic growth. **239**

97 Discuss the view that the costs of economic growth outweigh the benefits. **241**

98 Discuss the recent economic growth performance of the UK. **243**

Macroeconomic policy

Plan 99 Identify and explain the principal macroeconomic policy objectives. **247**

100 To what extent is it true that pursuit of one macroeconomic policy objective involves a trade-off in terms of the worsening of a different macroeconomic target? **249**

List of Abbreviations and Symbols **251**

Index **253**

List of figures

2.1 The production possibilities curve 13

4.1 Demand and supply 17

5.1 The market for beef 19

6.1 The effect of a maximum or ceiling price 23

6.2 The effect of a minimum or floor price 24

7.1 Excess demand 25

7.2 Excess supply 26

8.1 Inelastic demand 27

9.1 The market for motor cars 30

10.1 The effect of a unit tax on items with inelastic demand 31

10.2 Price elasticity varies along a straight-line demand curve 32

11.1 The long run in imperfect competition 35

12.1 Different elasticities of demand 37

12.2 Inelastic supply 38

12.3 The effect of an increase in demand 38

13.1 Increasing demand in the housing market 40

14.1 Normal and supernormal profit 41

15.1 The effect of a guaranteed (minimum) price 44

16.1 The effect of a minimum wage 45

17.1 Economic rent and transfer earnings 47

18.1 The effect of a tax on profits 49

19.1 The demand curve for labour 51

19.2 Skilled and unskilled wage rates 52

20.1 Marginal revenue product and wage rates 53

22.1 Average cost 59

23.1 Average fixed cost, average variable cost, and average total cost 61

25.1 The short run in perfect competition 67

25.2 The long run in perfect competition 68

26.1 Long-run equilibrium in perfect competition 69

26.2 Imperfect competition in the long run 70

27.1 Economies of large-scale production 71

28.1 Long-run equilibrium in imperfect competition 73

29.1 Structure–conduct–performance models 75

30.1 The kinked demand curve 77

32.1 Restriction of labour supply to raise wage levels 82

34.1 Consumers' surplus 85

34.2 Reduction in consumers' surplus 86

35.1 The case for monopoly 87

36.1 Price rigidity in oligopoly 89

37.1 The external costs of traffic congestion 93

40.1 Externalities 100

41.1 Income and wealth distribution curves 102

45.1 External costs of pollution 111

51.1 Aggregate demand and supply 128

53.1 The circular flow of income 131

54.1 Expenditure, income, and output 133

55.1 A consumption function 137

55.2 A consumption function where $C = a + bY$ 138

55.3 The Life-Cycle Hypothesis 138

56.1 Consumption as a function of income 139

59.1 Savings and investment 147

59.2 The savings function 147

60.1 Loanable funds 149

60.2 The marginal efficiency of capital 150

61.1 Investment and the marginal efficiency of capital 153

63.1 Equilibrium in the loanable funds market 158

63.2 A deflationary gap 158

65.1 The business cycle 163

67.1 Trade or business cycles 167

68.1 Inflationary and deflationary gaps 169

69.1 The effect of a contraction of the money supply 172

69.2 The effect of an expansion of the money supply 172

74.1 Liquidity preference curve 184

76.1 The Laffer Curve 190

78.1   The deflationary gap and national income 193

78.2   The inflationary gap and national income 194

79.1   Budget deficits and surpluses 195

82.1   An inflationary spiral 204

83.1   The natural rate of unemployment 205

84.1   The Phillips Curve 207

86.1   The effect of an increase in aggregate demand with a horizontal aggregate supply curve 213

86.2   The effect of an increase in aggregate demand with a vertical aggregate supply curve 214

87.1   The Phillips Curve relationship 215

90.1   Comparative advantage 223

91.1   The J-curve effect of devaluation 226

95.1   Floating exchange rate 236

95.2   Fixed exchange rate 236

Introduction

This collection of essay plans is intended to give only very basic outline answers to the questions posed. It is aimed at A-level and first-year undergraduate economics courses. Each plan can be used as the basis of a reasonable essay but it must be worked upon before it could possibly constitute a full response to the title. The plans are not 'model' answers. They provide a framework for one possible answer which needs to be added to and given some of your own writing style and flair. The plan does not have to be rigidly adhered to; it can be adapted to suit the interpretation you wish to give to your answer and it should certainly be added to in order to provide relevant up-to-date examples wherever this is possible. Most of the plans contain diagrams which are useful in explaining aspects of the essay. Other diagrams may also be relevant, or you may prefer to adapt the diagram to suit your interpretation of the essay.

The titles cover the most commonly asked questions on each syllabus area of microeconomics and macroeconomics.

Do not rely solely on the plan when writing your essay; further reading is necessary to give you a deeper insight into the nature of the problem and to enable you to write authoritatively about the subject. To this end, further reading is recommended with each plan. The references are to the following books:

Artis, M. J. (1996), *The UK Economy: A Manual of Applied Economics*, 14th edition (Oxford: Oxford University Press).

Beardshaw, J. (1992), *Economics: A Student's Guide*, 3rd edition (Wokingham: Addison-Wesley).

Lipsey, Richard G., and **Chrystal**, K. Alec (1995), *An Introduction to Positive Economics*, 8th edition (Oxford: Oxford University Press).

Parkin, M., **Powell**, M., and **Matthews**, K. (1997), *Economics* (Wokingham: Addison-Wesley).

Advice is given at the beginning to help you write good **coursework** essays. You should regard preparation work such as data collection as useful background reading and examination preparation.

The plans can be used as a **revision tool** for the essay paper of your examination. A useful revision tip is to summarize a plan in brief, then make it briefer and briefer still. Then try to expand it back to the original form without missing out key points.

Important advice for writing economics essays

Writing an essay involves responding to a question or title and takes the form of an argument which leads the reader from the title at the beginning to the conclusion at the end.

There is no set format for an essay in economics and there is certainly scope for you to introduce your own style. A commonly used and successful format, however, might look something like this:

1 Introduction
Lead into the essay by:
- defining terms used in the title   *or*
- setting the scene by discussing relevant topical issues

2 Main arguments or theories
Information section:
- make sure you attach most weight to (and give most space to) the most important argument or theory
- provide evidence for your argument
- keep to one main idea per paragraph
- use diagrams to illustrate the points you make
- where possible give real-world examples

3 Conclusion
Answer the question:
- stress the main points you have made
- avoid repeating yourself
- ensure that the conclusion is related to the rest of the essay

4 References
List the works to which you have referred (in alphabetical order). Each book reference should include in this order:
- surname, initial
- year of publication
- title
- place of publication
- publisher

Each article reference should include the title of the article, the title of the journal, the volume number, and the page numbers.

Essay techniques

It is important to write essays well because they continue to be an important means of assessment in economics. They help to clarify your ideas about a topic, to form arguments, and to identify what is relevant. They also help you to learn because you are more likely to remember something you have written about than something you have read about. Your essay ought to be written in good English because this will lead to greater clarity. You may not be penalized for grammatical errors or poor spelling but they create a bad impression which could reduce your final mark. Do not waffle. Your answer should be concise and relevant which means answering the question which has been set.

If you use **quotations** in an essay make sure that they add something to your answer; and try to avoid quoting verbatim really long passages of a piece of work.

Try to give your essay a **logical structure** which progresses from title to conclusion without doubling-back to points made earlier, or leaping from one topic to another which is completely different.

Use words in a way which demonstrates that you understand them. And when first referring to a concept give the reader enough information to understand what you mean. A good tip is to write as if you are addressing an intelligent but uninformed reader. Do not assume that the reader knows the meaning of technical terms.

If you draw heavily on the work of someone else (and you almost certainly will) then make sure that you acknowledge the source of the information either in the text, e.g. 'Keynes was the first to develop these ideas in *The General Theory of Employment, Interest and Money* (1936)' or simply '(Keynes 1936)' after the relevant point. In either case don't forget to include the reference at the end. If you do draw heavily on someone else's work—and this includes summarizing their ideas as well as using their exact words—and you do not acknowledge it, this is known as **plagiarism** and it is disapproved of in academic circles. It should certainly not be done at university level.

Finally, **style** is important. Be clear and concise and avoid overlong sentences. Avoid expressions such as 'I think that' or 'I believe' or, worst of all, 'I myself, personally, think that'. Better to say something like 'The evidence would seem to suggest that' or 'On the basis of the evidence available it would seem that'.

More advanced essay techniques

1 A general action sequence might help you to write a better essay. It might look like this:

(a) Gathering information: general research and note-making. Accurate and up-to-date information is the basis of an informative and well-written essay. You must first analyse the title in order to identify the information you need.

Make sure that you fully understand the terminology used in the title. You could look up the meaning of unfamiliar terms in a dictionary or encyclopaedia, or in an **economics dictionary** (of which there are two or three available). You will find a very useful **glossary of terms** in Parkin *et al.* (1997).

Don't leave the task until the last minute. Allow for problems, such as other students having the books you need, or a delay in reply to your letter requesting information from a company or local authority.

Use **newspaper sources** of information. There is a vast amount of economics information in the broadsheet daily newspapers. On the day after the Budget buy at least one of these plus the *Financial Times*—you will find facts and figures about the economy and public finance which are bang up to date and very comprehensive.

Be very clear about your research. It is possible to gather *too much* material and it is a mistake to try to put too much material into your essay. Continually ask if you need the information and if it adds to the quality (rather than the quantity) of your essay. If you found a lot of useful information early in your research, but not much from the sources found lately, it may be time to stop researching and start writing.

(b) Organizing information in a meaningful sequence (probably by writing an 'essay plan').

(c) Linking your paragraphs using linking sentences such as 'Having examined the major theories of influences on [subject] we will now turn to more subjective determinants.'

(d) Use statistics or diagrams to support your arguments and make your explanations clearer.

(e) Referencing: take care to reference information as you find it; it could save a lot of time at the end!

(f) Final presentation: word-processed or hand-written—either are acceptable to most tutors but if your handwriting is poor use a word processor!

2 A useful advanced essay technique would be to explore the underlying assumptions of the essay question. For example, if the title is 'Explain the distinction between private and social costs and the problems that can result when they diverge,' then the underlying assumptions are

(a) that private costs and social costs diverge;

(b) that the divergence causes problems.

Questions which should then be raised in the essay are

■ what are private costs?

■ what are social costs?

■ how do they differ?

■ what problems are caused by the divergence?

3 Use semi-independent paragraphs to construct your arguments. Within each paragraph you could question key assumptions of the essay and make claims or put forward theories for which you provide evidence.

4 Critically evaluate evidence put forward. This means that you should not accept evidence at face value. You should question whether the evidence is sound and scientifically based or likely to be biased. Collecting factual information is only part of the task. You may also be looking for data which confirm (or reject) a hypothesis in the title of the essay. You need to be able to **use the information** to interpret and evaluate the question or title. Be careful to look at both sides of the argument. For example you may believe that unemployment is a far bigger

problem than the rate of inflation, but don't be selective in the information you present. Make the case for both sides and use your conclusion to sum up the evidence the way you see it.

Be critical if you suspect bias in an argument or in evidence put forward. Give your reasons for suspecting bias and justify your criticisms.

5 Your conclusion should be relevant to the title and should summarize your arguments. Ideally it should follow logically from the main arguments or theories you put forward.

6 Use feedback on your essay to improve future essays.

What examiners are looking for

Some general characteristics which examiners will be assessing when they read your essay are listed here:
(a) knowledge of economic principles, concepts, and theories;
(b) knowledge of appropriate, relevant, and current information;
(c) ability to analyse the issues involved;
(d) well-presented material with supporting evidence;
(e) clear diagrams to illustrate relevant concepts;
(f) critical evaluation of material presented;
(g) ability to explain alternative views in order to reach a conclusion.

Use of the essay plans

Key concepts and features are printed in **bold type**. These will often need explaining in more detail. The diagrams which are used may need adapting and will certainly need further explanation.

Finally, when you have written your essay make sure that you read it. This will eliminate silly mistakes. I once had an essay from a student in which he'd written 'This will be referred to later in chapter 15'! Don't use subheadings, especially not 'Introduction', 'Main Arguments or Theories', etc. Your essay should flow from introduction to conclusion.

The plans contained in this book are intended as a guide only. They are not a substitute for the reading and preparation which must be done if you are to write clear, concise, and informative essays. They are a starting-point which should enable you to 'get into' the topic and a check to let you know that you are on the right lines. They must certainly be added to using your own knowledge and research—especially if the title does not precisely agree with the title you have been set. Remember, always answer the question; be relevant!

Further reading

Any introductory economics text will provide information on most of the topics covered in these essay plans: the books referred to in the Introduction are especially helpful.

Microeconomics

Introductory Microeconomics

'Economic theory has no practical value.' Discuss.

Introduction

Economics is the study of how society decides what, how, and for whom to produce. It is a science but because it is about human behaviour it is described as a **social science**. Economists aim to develop theories of human behaviour and to test them against the facts. Unlike pure sciences, such as physics, controlled experiments cannot be conducted in order to test the validity of an economic theory. As a result of the human element in any economic theory, a degree of unpredictability is likely and this leads to criticism from those who favour the techniques of pure science.

Main arguments or theories

Economic models are often used to provide an insight into economic problems. They are often criticized for making 'unrealistic' **assumptions** in order to simplify the economic situation. For example, in order to see how demand for bus journeys is affected by a change in fares it may be necessary to assume that passenger incomes, quality of buses, and other factors remain constant. Often the assumption **ceteris paribus** is used, which means **all other things being equal**, i.e. none of the other possible influences changes.

Often, when a long list of assumptions is made, as with the theory of **perfect competition**, students question the validity of the model being described. When faced with such a situation, Professor Joan Robinson of Cambridge University asked her students to consider what use a map would be on a scale of one to one! Economists first provide an explanation of a simplified version of reality and then gradually introduce complexity by relaxing the simplifying assumptions.

The scientific method of economics consists of the following stages:

- the observation of real-world events (facts)
- the identification of recurring general patterns
- the establishing of a body of explanation known as 'theory' in an attempt to explain the observed patterns
- the prediction of as yet unobserved events

This prediction of events must be where the practical value of economics lies. A useful theory will improve our knowledge of how the economy works. It makes realistic assumptions, has a logical and analytical basis, and makes predictions about economic behaviour which can be tested against **empirical evidence**.

Conclusion

Economic theories can seem to be very abstract and to be based on unrealistic assumptions. Their value can be seen when they provide reasonably accurate predictions of micro- or macroeconomic behaviour. The human or social element in economics means that predictions are liable to error; nevertheless economic theory provides a useful starting-point in attempts to control our economic environment and our economic future.

Further reading

→ Beardshaw, *chapter 1*
→ Lipsey and Chrystal, *chapter 2*
→ Parkin *et al.*, *chapter 1*

Explain how the concept of opportunity cost measures the real cost of resource allocation decisions.

Introduction

The central and defining problem in economics is that **resources** are **scarce** in relation to the demand for them. Because they are scarce they have alternative uses. For example labour and materials used to construct a road could have been used to build a hospital. The cost of the road is the opportunity forgone, the hospital. Thus the opportunity cost of any production decision is the loss of the next most desirable alternative.

Main arguments or theories

Opportunity costs can be illustrated using a **production possibilities curve (PPC)**:

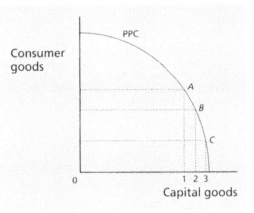

Figure 2.1 The production possibilities curve

Increasing production of capital goods from point 1 to point 2 involves a loss or opportunity cost of consumer goods from *A* to *B*. A similar increase in capital goods from point 2 to 3 involves a bigger opportunity cost of consumer goods from *B* to *C*. A PPC such as this one, which is concave to the origin, illustrates **increasing opportunity costs** as resources are transferred from production of one type of good to another.

Prices will reflect opportunity costs if no **market imperfections** such as taxes or monopoly profits exist and there is no divergence between **private costs** and **social costs** (arising from **externalities**). Opportunity costs are thus the real costs of economic decisions as long as market imperfections are minimized. Where there is considerable divergence between private and social costs, then **social opportunity costs** may have to be measured using the techniques of **cost-benefit analysis**.

Conclusion

The concept of opportunity cost is a more accurate measure of costs (in terms of forgone alternatives) than are firms' costs (in terms of input prices). Where there are significant market imperfections, however, the concept of social opportunity cost may have to be employed in order to measure the real costs of an economic activity.

Further reading

→ Beardshaw, *chapter 3*
→ Lipsey and Chrystal, *pp. 5–6 and 185–8*
→ Parkin *et al.*, *chapter 3*

Outline the essential differences between free-market and centrally planned economies. Discuss the economic problems which may arise in the transition of the Eastern European economies to the market system.

Introduction

Most economies in the world are **mixed economies** with elements of both central planning and free markets. The nearest examples of free-market economies where **government intervention** is kept to a minimum are the USA and Japan, although even there the **public sector** is responsible for about 30 per cent of GDP. The nearest examples of centrally planned economies were the countries of Eastern Europe and the former Soviet Union. These countries are now making the transition to market systems while China, theoretically the world's largest centrally planned or **command economy**, is increasingly allowing **market forces** to allocate resources.

Main arguments or theories

In a free market economy, **prices** act as 'signals' to producers to indicate what to produce and where to allocate resources. In a centrally planned economy, decisions regarding production, distribution, and exchange of goods and services are made by bureaucrats or planners. The free-market system is very efficient, with market prices bringing about equilibrium between demand and supply of commodities. In a centrally planned system, the accuracy of the production plans is not guaranteed and shortages and surpluses can arise.

Private ownership of resources and production for **profit** are key features of free-market economies, whereas in centrally planned economies **collective ownership** of the factors of production means that there may be a lack of incentives to work and produce and a lack of **entrepreneurial spirit**.

The change from a planned economy to a free-market economy will inevitably lead to disruption. Workers who were employed in state factories may no longer have a job and therefore no spending power. Factories may find it difficult to secure

Introductory Microeconomics   **15**

supplies which were once guaranteed by the state. Markets for vital commodities may not exist. Where shortages arise, **black markets** may develop with prices beyond the reach of ordinary people. It seems inevitable that for many people in these countries, living standards will fall for at least the transition period.

Capital markets to raise funds for **investment** do not exist, which makes future economic growth slower and dependent upon foreign investment. Lack of **entrepreneurs** will also hamper future performance. The transition from state-subsidized prices to free-market prices will be inflationary and put many commodities beyond the reach of most people, whose incomes will be slow to rise because of the slow pace of growth.

Conclusion

The argument that greater efficiency and more rapid rates of growth are possible with free-market systems appears to have been won with the transition of the former USSR and Eastern Europe to a **free-enterprise economy**. For several years, however, the problems of adjusting to a new system are likely to suppress living standards and economic growth. However, at some point the dynamism of the free-enterprise system should lead to a rise in GDP, which can be sustained and which will improve living standards.

Further reading

→ Artis, *p. 17*
→ Beardshaw, *chapter 5*
→ Lipsey and Chrystal, *chapter 1*
→ Parkin *et al., chapter 1*

Discuss the role of the price mechanism in the allocation of economic resources.

Introduction

Economic resources are scarce relative to the demand for them and this means that **choices** have to be made. In a free-market economy (and to a large extent in a mixed economy) these decisions are made automatically by **market forces** operating through the price mechanism. Adam Smith in the *Wealth of Nations* (1786) described this automatic allocation system as the **'invisible hand'** which miraculously moved the resources to where they were wanted.

Main arguments or theories

The market system determines what, how, and for whom goods and services are produced. The consumer determines 'what' to produce (**consumer sovereignty**). An increase in consumer demand will lead to a rise in price and producers will respond to the higher price by raising production (to make more profits). Competition between producers determines 'how' to produce—if they do not produce as cheaply as possible they will go out of business. 'For whom' to produce is decided by prices in factor markets. Some people have high incomes because their skills are scarce and they can then afford more resources.

Figure 4.1 explains how an increase in demand will lead to a rise in price, which acts as the **signal** to reallocate resources:

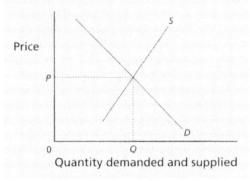

Figure 4.1 Demand and supply

A useful example is that of a farmer growing two crops, one of which is in increasing demand, the other in decreasing demand. As the price of the one rises and the other falls it is easy to see that he will reallocate fields to the production of the crop whose demand is increasing and reduce the number of fields allocated to the crop whose demand is falling.

There are areas where the price mechanism does not give an optimal solution, however. These areas are known as instances of **market failure**. They occur for the following reasons:

- **public goods**, such as law and order and defence, may not be provided;
- **merit goods**, such as education and health care, may be underprovided;
- **social costs (and benefits)**, known as **externalities** or spillover effects, may not be taken into account by market prices, e.g. pollution of the atmosphere by a firm's emissions may not be paid for or compensated for.

Conclusion

The price mechanism is a very efficient method of resource allocation which allows the consumer to express his/her preferences through prices which act as signals to producers. There are, however, areas of the economy which require government intervention because the price system does not work properly where there is market failure.

Further reading

→ Beardshaw, *chapter 8*
→ Lipsey and Chrystal, *chapter 4*
→ Parkin *et al.*, *chapter 4*

Compare and contrast the principal economic characteristics of a free-market economy with those of a planned economy.

Introduction

In a free-market economy, the allocation of resources is determined by the actions of consumers and producers in markets, whereas in a centrally planned or command economy, economic behaviour is determined by a central authority. In practice there are few examples of planned economies in the world since the collapse of this system in the former Soviet Union, and in fact all economies are mixed economies having elements of free markets and central planning but often to a different degree.

Main arguments or theories

In a free-market economy an **invisible hand** seems to guide the system so that the outcome of millions of independent decisions made by producers and consumers leads neither to vast surpluses nor persistent shortages.

Prices act as signals to producers to indicate what to produce and where to allocate resources. A market price is the result of the interaction of consumers' demand and producers' supply, where the wishes of buyers and sellers coincide:

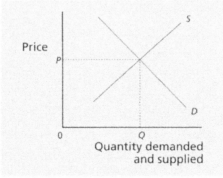

Figure 5.1 The market for beef

A change in consumer tastes, for example away from beef (perhaps because of a health scare), would lead to a shift to the left of the demand curve, which would result in a fall in market price. Producers would respond to the fall in price by re-allocating resources to more profitable areas of production.

Central to free-market economic systems is the legal right of individuals to buy, own, and dispose of land, building, and machines; to hire the services of labour; and to undertake production with a view to **profit**.

The main disadvantages of the free-market economy are

- unequal distribution of wealth
- instability (cyclical patterns of boom and slump)
- monopolies can develop
- certain non-market services may not be provided, e.g. law and order
- other **merit goods** may be underprovided, e.g. education, health

In a centrally planned economy decisions regarding production, distribution, and exchange of goods and services are made by the all-powerful central authority. The efficiency of this economic system depends on the accuracy of the centrally made plans. Collective ownership of factors of production means that there will be no personal income in the form of rent interest and profit. The main problems with this system are

- without prices to act as signals, mistakes are often made in the allocation of resources
- the people doing the planning are themselves 'wasted resources' and a large bureaucracy is likely

Conclusion

In reality all economies contain elements of free markets and central planning and are **mixed economies**. Most world economies can now be described as 'free-market economies regulated by government'.

Further reading

→ Beardshaw, *chapter 5*
→ Lipsey and Chrystal, *chapter 1*

Demand and supply analysis

Why might government intervention, in the form of price ceilings and floors, have undesirable consequences?

Introduction

Either

(1) this could be topical in that **minimum wage legislation** was a key area of political debate in the 1992 and 1997 general elections, while **maximum rents** have been accused of reducing the stock of rented accommodation (90 per cent of dwellings in 1914; approximately 12 per cent in 1980),

or

(2) your introduction could discuss one of the central issues in economics: **intervention** versus **non-intervention**. In general, free-market economists believe that the market works best if left to itself (**laissez-faire**) while interventionists believe that the problems of free-market economics mean that significant intervention is necessary.

Main arguments or theories

Effect of maximum price control (a price ceiling)
- explanation of how a ceiling price leads to excess demand:

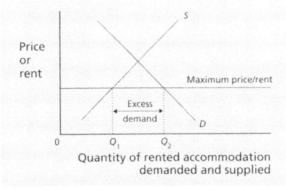

Figure 6.1 The effect of a maximum or ceiling price

- resulting problems: waiting lists, queues, sellers' preferences, black-market transactions
- relevant legislation: 1965 Rent Act; 1974 Rent Act

Effect of minimum price control (a floor price)

- explanation of how a floor price leads to excess supply:

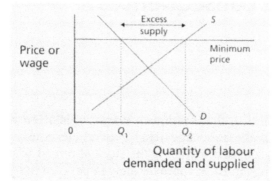

Figure 6.2 The effect of a minimum or floor price

- excess supply of labour means unemployment
- resulting problems: implications for public finance, economic growth, and social effects

Note that this analysis could be applied to farm prices and overproduction.

Conclusion

Your own interpretation of the success or otherwise of government intervention in the market.

Further reading

→ Beardshaw, *chapter 11*
→ Lipsey and Chrystal, *chapter 6*
→ Parkin *et al., chapter 6*

'Price controls are an inefficient method of helping poor people because they always lead to shortages.' Discuss.

Introduction

Governments intervene in markets in order to protect those people who are on low incomes and who may not be able to afford basic essentials such as housing or food. The form of intervention may be a maximum or ceiling price which the government believes is affordable and an example would be rent controls (introduced in Britain during World War I). Minimum wage legislation is a form of price control which also aims to help those who are on low incomes, but by raising those incomes rather than by controlling the price of the things they buy.

Main arguments or theories

Show the effect of a ceiling price leading to **excess demand** and a housing shortage:

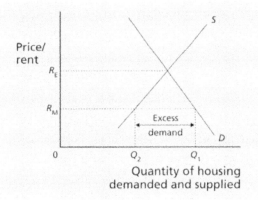

Figure 7.1 Excess demand

Explain that the consequences of the policy may be
- queueing
- waiting lists
- rationing of some form
- black-market prices/rents being charged illegally

Minimum wage legislation to improve the lot of the low paid may have the opposite effect, however:

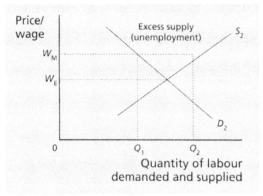

Figure 7.2 Excess supply

Explain the consequences of **Wage Councils** in the UK and other minimum wage legislation in Europe and the US and its effects on unskilled workers and older workers.

Conclusion

Maximum price control will lead to shortages, as shown by Fair Rents legislation in the UK. Minimum price legislation, however, which is another form of price control, will lead to surpluses which may be the result of minimum wage legislation (leading to unemployment) although there are those who argue that this is not necessarily the case.

Further reading

→ Beardshaw, *chapter 11*
→ Lipsey and Chrystal, *chapter 6*
→ Parkin *et al.*, *chapter 6*

With reference to examples, explain the use that economists make of the concepts of price elasticity of demand and income elasticity of demand.

Introduction

Elasticity is an important concept in economics which is used to describe how one variable, such as quantity demanded, responds to a change in another, such as price or income. **Price elasticity of demand (PED)** is given by the expression

$$PED = \frac{\text{percentage change in quantity demanded}}{\text{percentage change in price}}$$

while **income elasticity of demand (YED)** is given by the expression

$$YED = \frac{\text{percentage change in quantity demanded}}{\text{percentage change in income}}$$

Main arguments or theories

PED is extremely important to firms in deciding on their pricing strategy. A firm facing inelastic demand over its immediate price range can raise its price and increase its revenue:

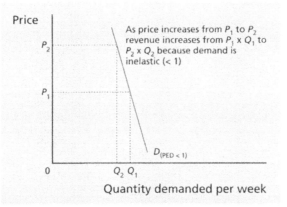

Figure 8.1 Inelastic demand

Conversely, a firm which has elastic demand over its immediate price range would lose revenue if it raised its price.

This concept is also of great importance to governments when considering their indirect taxation strategy. Levying indirect taxes will raise most revenue for government if those taxes are applied to goods with inelastic demand, because the demand for them will not fall significantly after the price rise. In the UK, petrol, alcohol, and tobacco provide examples of such goods.

Information on income elasticity of demand would be of use to firms when considering their product strategy, particularly over the longer term. If *YED* is elastic (greater than 1) then an increase in consumer incomes, which could be expected during a period of economic growth, will lead to a more than proportionate increase in demand for the product. Luxury goods tend to exhibit high income elasticity of demand and are described as **income-elastic**.

Conversely there are some goods and services for which demand does not increase greatly when incomes increase, examples being foodstuffs and cleaning materials.

Some goods and services may even be **inferior**, demand for them actually falling when incomes increase. Examples here may be bus journeys and cheap low-quality foods.

Conclusion

Economists use the concepts of price elasticity of demand and income elasticity of demand to show how firms make decisions on pricing and product strategy and how governments can use the information to guide policy on indirect taxation.

Further reading

→ Beardshaw, *chapter 10*
→ Lipsey and Chrystal, *chapter 5*
→ Parkin *et al.*, *chapter 5*

Examine the main influences on the price of motor cars.

Introduction

Either

(1) provide a brief explanation of demand and supply interaction, equilibrium price, and market clearing

or

(2) a more specific introduction stressing the increased availability of motor cars, and the impact of mass production on prices, making cars more affordable to more people in the developed world.

Main arguments or theories

■ Show elements of demand in a **demand function**, e.g.

$$Q_D = f(P; P_{1\ldots n}, t, Y, Pop^n)$$

where

Q_D = quantity demanded
f = is a function of
P = price
$P_{1\ldots n}$ = prices of other goods (complements and substitutes)
t = tastes
Y = income
Pop^n = population size and composition

Relate each of the constituent parts of the demand function to the motor-car market (e.g. public transport is a **substitute** for private-car purchase).

■ Show elements of supply in a **supply function**, e.g.

$$Q_S = f(P; P_{F1\ldots n}, T_Y)$$

where

Q_S = quantity supplied
f = is a function of

P = price

$P_{FI...n}$ = prices of factors of production

T_Y = level of technology

Relate each of the constituent parts of the supply function to the motor-car market (e.g. steel is a factor of production in car manufacturing).

■ Show how demand and supply curves intersect to give an equilibrium price and quantity:

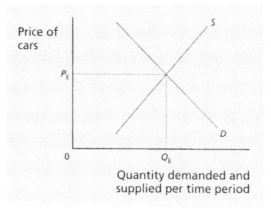

Figure 9.1 The market for motor cars

■ Explain how a change in a **factor affecting supply** or a **factor affecting demand** will affect the equilibrium price (e.g. a rise in the price of steel will shift the supply curve to the left, causing the price of cars to rise).

Conclusion

Give your assessment of the main factors affecting supply and demand in the motor-car industry.

Further reading

→ Beardshaw, *chapter 5*

→ Lipsey and Chrystal, *chapter 4*

→ Parkin *et al.*, *chapter 4*

Examine the significance of price elasticity of demand in decisions relating to an increase in the tax on tobacco.

Introduction

In the UK, taxes on tobacco are a significant percentage of the final purchase price of the product—some 80 per cent in the case of a packet of cigarettes. The tax is mainly a **lump sum tax** per unit (per packet) although Value Added Tax (VAT) is also applied. This results in a total tax yield from tobacco of approximately £7.7 billion for the government (1996), which is about 3 per cent of all taxation.

Main arguments or theories

Cigarette and tobacco duty is usually increased each year in the **Budget** at least in line with inflation and often by more in an attempt to discourage its use. This is because tobacco is regarded as a **demerit good** (or **merit bad**) with harmful effects and it is felt that under a **laissez-faire** policy more tobacco would be used than is socially desirable.

The government has a dilemma, however, since if it discourages smoking too much then it loses a significant source of revenue. Demand for tobacco is considered to be **inelastic** because of the absence of **substitutes** and the habit-forming nature of the product. An increase in the excise duty on tobacco will lead to an increase in revenue for government because of this inelastic demand:

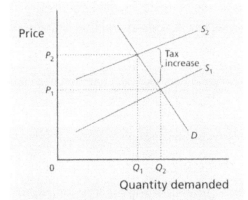

Figure 10.1 The effect of a unit tax on items with inelastic demand

Despite the significant tax increase, the quantity demanded falls by relatively little from Q_1 to Q_2.

Price elasticity of demand (*PED*) varies, however, along a demand curve and it may be that there will come a time when the price rises to the point where the demand curve for tobacco is no longer inelastic:

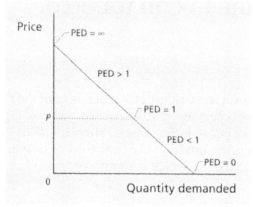

Figure 10.2 Price elasticity varies along a straight-line demand curve

If the tax increase pushes the price above *P* in Figure 10.2 then there will be a reduction in revenue for the government because *PED* is now elastic (greater than 1).

Conclusion

If the sole objective of the government in taxing tobacco is to raise revenue then great care should be taken to avoid increasing the tax and price to the point where *PED* is greater than 1 (elastic). It is more likely, however, that the government also have health objectives in mind when decisions are taken on tobacco duties, and this seems to be confirmed by the increased duties in recent Budgets which have resulted in proportionately less revenue, suggesting greater elasticity of demand for tobacco.

Further reading

→ Artis, *pp. 216–17*
→ Beardshaw, *chapter 10*
→ Lipsey and Chrystal, *chapter 5*
→ Parking *et al., chapter 5*

Markets

Critically discuss the view that advertising promotes market imperfection and is against the interests of consumers.

Introduction

Advertising is one of the methods of **non-price competition** which can occur in **imperfect competition** and in **oligopoly**. In theory it should not occur in a situation of pure monopoly because the firm has no competition. In reality, however, even firms with a monopoly may advertise to bring their product to the attention of consumers, or to try to enlarge their market, or to consolidate their market position.

Main arguments or theories

Non-price competition raises costs in firms in the market structure of **imperfect competition**. This leads to an allocative inefficiency known as **excess capacity**.

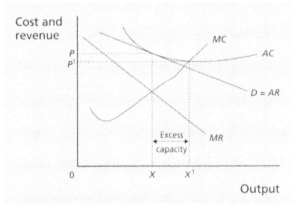

Figure 11.1 The long run in imperfect competition

Because price P is higher than the perfectly competitive price of P^1 would be, and output X is lower than the perfectly competitive output of X^1 would be, non-price competition, including advertising, is deemed to be inefficient.

It can be argued that since advertising does not directly satisfy consumers' wants, it is a waste of resources. But advertising does provide consumers with information about how products differ and as a result consumers can make a better product choice.

Conclusion

It is clear that some advertising is a waste of resources and raises firms' costs, which is inefficient. In some markets, however, it is possible that the gains from extra product variety outweigh the costs of advertising and excess capacity. The large variety of foods, magazines, and soft drinks provide examples of such gains.

Further reading

→ Beardshaw, *chapter 17*
→ Lipsey and Chrystal, *chapter 14*
→ Parkin *et al.*, *chapter 13*

Why do manufactured goods typically exhibit greater price stability than is the case with primary products?

Introduction

Primary products are agricultural products and mineral products which are extracted and traded without being manufactured. Their supply is subject to large variations, often resulting from factors beyond human control, such as bad weather or the exhaustion of a mineral deposit. Further instability can arise on the demand side as demand curves for most products are affected by business activity, rising in a boom and falling in a recession.

Main arguments or theories

Primary products tend to have **inelastic demands**, which means that unplanned changes in production (**supply shocks**) will lead to large fluctuations in price.

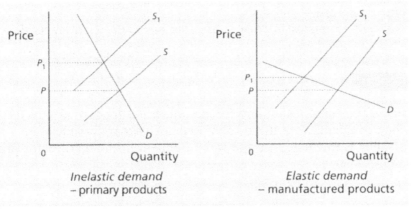

Figure 12.1 **Different elasticities of demand**

The inelasticity of demand for agricultural and other primary products is because they are essential commodities and they often comprise only a small proportion of the price of a final product.

Cyclical instability can lead to **shifts in demand** for primary products. In periods of prosperity, incomes are high and demand increases, while in a recession, incomes fall and demand is lower. These shifts in demand also lead to large price changes, especially as they take place on relatively **inelastic supply** curves:

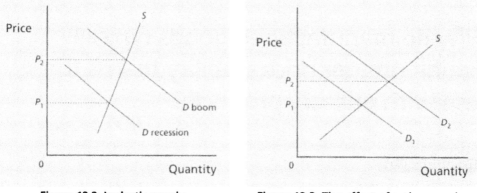

Figure 12.2 Inelastic supply

Figure 12.3 The effect of an increase in demand

Supply of manufactured goods is more **elastic** than that of primary products. If business managers want to increase supply of manufactures they can introduce overtime, or a night shift, or expand their premises—all relatively straightforward compared with planting new fields or opening new mines.

Also, manufactured goods tend to have many substitutes, making the demand for them more elastic also. Hatchback cars are a good example—if the price of one make rises, then many sales are likely to be lost to rivals.

Where both demand and supply curves are elastic, a shift in either is unlikely to lead to a large change in price. For example, if demand for manufactures increases in an economic upturn—
—there is a relatively modest increase in price because of the relatively elastic supply.

Conclusion

Both demand and supply conditions for manufactured goods tend to be relatively elastic when compared with those conditions for primary products. As a result price instability is much greater and more frequent in the markets for primary commodities.

Further reading

→ Beardshaw, *chapters 10 and 12*
→ Lipsey and Chrystal, *chapter 6*
→ Parkin *et al., chapter 5*

Examine the factors which could be expected to determine the price of houses in a free market.

Introduction

In neo-classical economic theory, **demand** and **supply** establish the **equilibrium price** and quantity of any product. In the market for housing for owner-occupation, however, that equilibrium is difficult to establish because of the unique nature of each house, flat, cottage, or bungalow. Non-monetary factors may influence house prices, such as area or schools, and house prices can vary widely geographically because of the uneven spread of job opportunities.

Main arguments or theories

Generally, the price of new houses will be determined by existing house prices—because of the durability of buildings the supply of houses is dominated by the existing stock (new building contributes only about 1.1 per cent per year). Because of this the supply of houses is relatively **inelastic** even over a long period and price changes are therefore caused by demand changes.

There are many influences on demand for houses to buy. Some of the most important are: **incomes** of households, the **mortgage rate**, the rate of **household formation**, the availability of **rental accommodation**, and **expectations of future prices**.

During the 1980s, the increased tendency to divorce led to increased rates of household formation, while in the mid-to-late 1980s incomes grew rapidly. In addition, changes to **financial markets** through **deregulation** in 1987 made mortgages cheaper and easier to obtain. These factors led to a **house price boom** between 1986 and 1988 which is illustrated on p. 40:

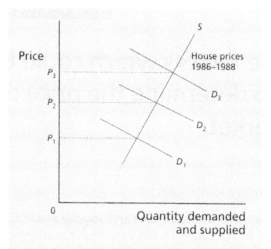

Figure 13.1 Increasing demand in the housing market

The nature of housing supply ensured that the supply of houses could not keep up with the rapidly increasing demand and the result was a rapid increase in prices.

Conclusion

There are many different characteristics of a house which complicate analysis of the housing market. Nevertheless the demand and supply of houses will deter-mine the equilibrium price of broadly similar types of house. The main influences on supply are the existing stock of houses, land costs (and planning restrictions), building costs, and the time taken in construction. The main influences on demand are incomes, the mortgage rate, the rate of household formation, and the availability of substitute rental accommodation.

Further reading

→ Beardshaw, *chapter 8*
→ Lipsey and Chrystal, *chapters 4 and 6*
→ Parkin *et al.*, *chapter 6*

Explain what is meant by the terms 'normal profit' and 'supernormal' or 'abnormal profit'.

Introduction

To an accountant, profit is revenue in excess of costs, whereas to an economist revenue in excess of **opportunity costs** is **supernormal profit**. The distinction is that an entrepreneur is likely to have opportunities to pursue alternative activities to that which s/he is currently in and so part of the profit is compensation for remaining in the present activity. So **normal profit** is the minimum amount of profit which is necessary to keep the firm in the industry, while supernormal profit is any excess of profit beyond that.

Main arguments or theories

The concepts of normal and supernormal profit can be simply illustrated:

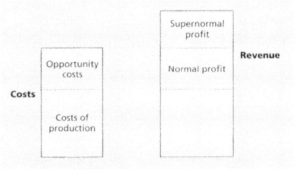

Figure 14.1 Normal and supernormal profit

To an economist, normal profit is considered a cost of production and it is included in the firm's average costs. Entrepreneurs can calculate their likely earnings in another occupation or venture before beginning production, and so normal profit can be considered a fixed cost. Because entrepreneurs do not all have equal ability or expectations, the level of normal profit will vary from industry to industry. Moreover, the level of **risk** involved will vary and an industry with high risk will require a greater amount of normal profit.

In the market form of **perfect competition**, abnormal or supernormal profits will only be possible in the short run because the entry of new firms, attracted by the high profits, will compete away any returns above normal profit. Entry will cease when price has fallen to a level which only allows normal profit. It may be possible for firms to earn supernormal profits for a while because it takes time for new firms to enter the industry because of construction or other delays. Such temporary profits are known as **quasi-rents**, which are the result of short-term fixed supply of factors of production.

By contrast, in the market form of **monopoly**, supernormal profits can continue in the long run because there are barriers to the entry of new firms.

Conclusion

Economists regard a part of revenue in excess of costs as the opportunity cost of being in a particular activity. It is equal to the entrepreneur's assessment of his/her earnings or return from an alternative venture. As a consequence only revenue in excess of opportunity costs and conventional costs is regarded as supernormal or abnormal profit.

Further reading

→ Beardshaw, *chapter 14*
→ Lipsey and Chrystal, *chapter 10*

Explain the reasons for and the effects of government or European Union support for agriculture.

Introduction

There are two main reasons why governments in most developed countries intervene in agricultural markets. First, they attempt to **stabilize prices** because both supply and demand for agricultural products are **price-inelastic** so that small changes in either demand or supply will result in relatively large changes in equilibrium prices. Secondly, **farm incomes** tend to be volatile because prices are volatile and with inelastic demand, farmers can receive higher incomes when crops are poor and lower incomes when crops are good.

Main arguments or theories

Agricultural markets are liable to short-run instability arising from sudden **supply shocks** which can be caused by climate changes. Moreover, demand can fluctuate considerably with the trade cycle, and because supply is inelastic this will result in large price changes.

The European Union has provided support for agriculture for more than thirty years through its **Common Agricultural Policy** (**CAP**). The main method of support involves maintaining a market price for many agricultural products which is higher than the price in the rest of the world. The high prices are maintained by protection against cheaper imports and by **intervention buying** of the surpluses that result from the excess supply:

Markets   **43**

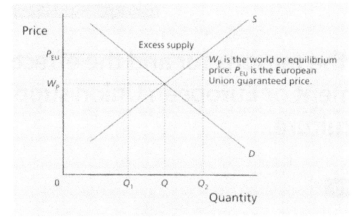

Figure 15.1 The effect of a guaranteed (minimum) price

Intervention buying, however, has led to build-ups of surpluses, which have become known as grain mountains, beef mountains, wine lakes, milk lakes, etc. They are eventually disposed of by selling them to a non-EU country at a reduced subsidized price (a process known as **dumping**) or even destroyed. This is done so that they cannot be resold on to the EU market.

As predicted by economic theory, greater and greater surplus production must be bought and disposed of by the EU and the costs of doing so have caused great controversy as they rose until, in 1988, reforms were made, including the controversial 'set-aside' policy, which provides payments to farmers for leaving up to 15 per cent of their land fallow.

A further consequence of guaranteed prices has been the pursuit of higher and higher yields by more intensive farming and increased use of fertilizers. This has had enormous **environmental consequences** for landscape, water quality, and wildlife.

Conclusion

European Union agricultural policies have created surpluses of agricultural products in Europe and caused financial crises for the EU. Food prices to consumers in Europe have been higher than they need to be. Both of these results could have been predicted by microeconomic theory. More fundamental consequences for the environment are also the result of the pursuit of higher yields.

Further reading

→ Beardshaw, *chapter 12*
→ Lipsey and Chrystal, *chapter 6*
→ Parkin *et al.*, *chapter 6*

Discuss the view that minimum wage legislation will lead to increased unemployment.

Introduction

Economists disagree about the effects of minimum wage legislation. Many argue that as with any **floor price** it will lead to **excess supply**, which in this case means **unemployment**. Others argue that the labour market is not like product markets and, if wages are generally low, the increased wage level may actually increase the incentive to work among those who are unemployed and living on benefits.

Main arguments or theories

The demand for labour is a **derived demand**: it is demanded not for itself but for the goods and services it produces. Under competitive conditions labour will be employed to the point where the wage rate equals the **marginal revenue product (MRP)** of labour (the value of the output of the last worker employed). The MRP curve slopes downwards to the right because as employment expands, output increases and the price of the product will fall. The MRP curve can be considered to be the demand curve for labour.

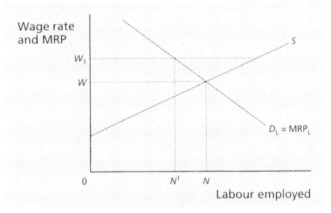

Figure 16.1 The effect of a minimum wage

It can be seen from the diagram that an increase in the wage rate from W to W_1 will reduce employment from N to N_1 and this is the traditional or classical view of minimum wage laws.

In **monopsonistic labour markets** (where the employer is the only employer of labour in the area), however, the firm becomes a price-taker and it cannot exercise its monopsony power. Moreover, there is no point in the firm trying to drive the wage rate down by reducing its demand for labour, and in these circumstances both wages and employment can be raised to the competitive level.

Conclusion

In practice, minimum wage legislation has limited effects. It has been introduced in the United States and Canada and in many European countries. The occupations affected are obviously those with the lowest pay and they are unskilled or semi-skilled. Some groups, especially the young or minority groups, are affected more than others. Minimum wage legislation can succeed in raising the wages of employed workers, but there is a risk of higher unemployment, particularly among the young and the unskilled.

Further reading

→ Beardshaw, *chapter 11*
→ Lipsey and Chrystal, *chapter 19*
→ Parkin *et al.*, *chapter 6*

Explain why it is sometimes argued that taxes should be imposed upon economic rents.

Introduction

Any excess which a **factor of production** earns over the minimum amount needed to keep it in its present use is called its **economic rent**. It was first described by the great British economist David Ricardo as the return to a factor of production which is in fixed supply, such as land.

Main arguments or theories

The minimum payment which is necessary to keep a factor of production in its present use is known as its **transfer earnings**. Where the factor has particularly high earnings in one particular use, the excess of earnings over whatever it could earn in another use could be considerable.

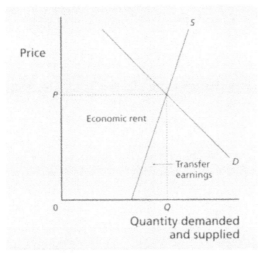

Figure 17.1 Economic rent and transfer earnings

An example would be a highly paid entertainer (whose earnings in any other occupation would be considerably less) or land with planning permission for building or any depletable (or non-renewable) resource such as oil.

Wherever the demand curve is **inelastic** it should be obvious that the economic rent will be considerable. It is often argued that this excess of earnings over the transfer earnings can be taxed without affecting the **allocation of resources**. If earnings in any other occupation or use are very low then even high taxes will not change the usage of the factor of production, as long as the government only take the economic rent and do not tax the transfer earnings.

There are, however, serious practical difficulties in identifying the element of pure economic rent in a factor's earnings. In the UK, Capital Gains Tax and North Sea Oil Royalties attempt to do this.

Conclusion

The taxation of economic rents was first advocated on land, which is fixed in supply, and which appears to give 'unearned' income to landowners (because the returns or rent can rise without any extra effort by the landowner). It is an attractive proposition because a tax of this nature would not affect the allocation of resources, which makes it **economically efficient**. There are serious practical difficulties, however, in identifying that portion of earnings which is economic rent.

Further reading

→ Beardshaw, *chapter 22*
→ Lipsey and Chrystal, *pp. 342–5*
→ Parkin *et al., chapter 14*

Discuss the view that company profit is an unnecessary surplus which should be removed by the imposition of high taxes.

Introduction

Profit is the difference between the revenue the firm gains from selling its output minus the cost of producing that output. Firms in competitive markets can in the long run only make **normal profit** (which covers the costs of production plus the opportunity costs of capital), which is just sufficient to keep the firm in business. Any excess of revenue over normal profit is known as **supernormal profit**.

Main arguments or theories

It is thought that a tax levied on supernormal profits will have no effect on price and output in any market structure. In perfect competition, there are no supernormal profits in the long run and firms will pay no profits tax. A tax on company profits, therefore, will not affect the long-run behaviour of firms in perfect competition.

In monopoly, firms earn supernormal profits in the long run and would therefore pay profits tax. The tax would reduce the firm's profits but would not alter its price or output decisions.

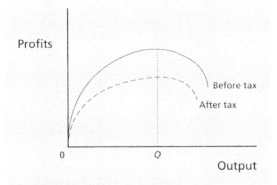

Figure 18.1 The effect of a tax on profits

In Figure 18.1 a percentage tax on profits (such as UK Corporation Tax, currently 29–35 per cent, depending on the size of the firm) shifts the 'Before tax' curve downwards but the profit-maximizing output remains at Q.

In practice, taxes on firms' profits are applied to profits as defined by accountants rather than economists and they include the return on capital and the reward for **enterprise** or risk-taking (which economists regard as a cost). A tax on profits as they are defined for tax purposes will therefore have an effect on price and output decisions and the allocation of resources. Firms may avoid the tax on profits by **'ploughing back'** or reinvesting those profits in the business rather than distributing them.

Profits are important to the **free-enterprise** economy, however, because they provide the incentive to take the risk of innovation and production. Entrepreneurs who are able to earn high profits because of their exceptional abilities create **employment** and **incomes** and contribute to **higher rates of economic growth**; to remove their incentive completely would be folly.

Conclusion

Profit is the driving force of a free-enterprise economy, giving incentive to entrepreneurs to invest, to innovate, to invest, to produce, and above all, to take **risks**. A tax on supernormal profit ought not to affect the allocation of resources but care must be taken not to damage incentives.

Further reading:

→ Beardshaw, *chapter 24*
→ Lipsey and Chrystal, *pp. 285–6*
→ Parkin *et al.*, *chapter 14*

Assess the validity of the marginal productivity theory of wages in explaining wage levels in the United Kingdom.

Introduction

Wage levels in the UK are influenced by a number of factors, including trade union membership, government intervention in labour markets, and levels of productivity (output per worker). The marginal productivity theory of wages suggests that labour is employed to the point where the wage rate is equal to the **marginal revenue product** of labour.

Main arguments or theories

Explain **marginal physical product** and **marginal revenue product** (**MRP**). The demand curve for labour is that part of the marginal revenue product curve below the average revenue product curve (ARP).

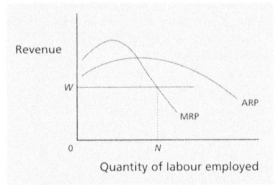

Figure 19.1 The demand curve for labour

At a wage rate of W, N workers are employed. Each worker up to N adds more revenue to the firm than his wage—additional workers beyond N would add more to the wage bill than to revenue.

The demand for labour is a **derived demand**—it depends on the productivity of the workforce. Note that if productivity were to increase (i.e. the MRP curve were to shift upwards) more workers could be employed *or* the wage rate could rise.

Problems with the theory:

- workers are not homogeneous; in particular, skill levels vary
- in general skilled workers have higher wages than unskilled:

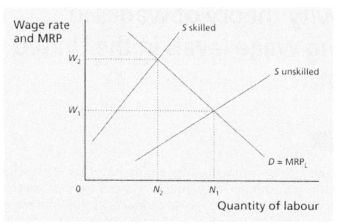

Figure 19.2 Skilled and unskilled wage rates

- MRP is difficult to calculate, especially in service industries (explain)
- government legislation such as the Equal Pay Act 1970 and any form of minimum wage legislation will affect wage rates.

Conclusion

Wages are the price of labour and will be determined by the interaction of supply and demand. The marginal productivity theory of wages is a theory of demand for labour. The supply of labour will also affect wage levels and is affected by skill levels and the strength of trade unions.

Further reading

→ Artis, *pp. 315–21*

→ Beardshaw, *chapter 21*

→ Lipsey and Chrystal, *chapter 18*

→ Parkin *et al., chapter 15*

Evaluate the success of equal pay legislation in raising women's wages.

Introduction

Equal pay legislation was introduced in the UK in 1970, with the intention of ending discrimination against women in terms of wages and fringe benefits or 'perks'. The Equal Pay Act of 1970 and the Sex Discrimination Act of 1975 came fully into force in 1976, making it illegal for employers to pay men more than women for doing identical jobs (although the fact that it is illegal does not mean that it never happens!).

Main arguments or theories

Firms regard female workers as having a lower **marginal revenue product (MRP)** than men and they employ labour until the MRP equals the wage rate.

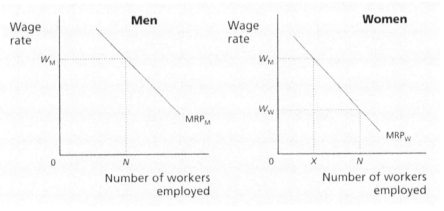

Figure 20.1 Marginal revenue product and wage rates

In the diagrams, if the female wage rate is W_W, which is lower than the men's W_M, then equal numbers of men and women (N) will be employed. If wage rates are equal and employers perceive the marginal revenue product of women to be lower than men (MRP_W) then women's employment will fall to X.

Reasons why employers might perceive women's MRP to be less than men's:

- women's attachment to the labour force is weaker than mens
- 40 per cent of female employment is part-time (5 per cent for men)
- labour turnover is higher for females in most industries (higher costs for firms)

- spells out of employment mean that women's training is interrupted and career progression is disjointed
- absenteeism is higher for women

Conclusion

Despite equal pay legislation in the 1970s, wage rates for women in Britain tend, on average, to be only 65–70 per cent of those of men. The main reason for this is the perception of employers that women have lower productivity than men for the reasons listed above and because many women work in low-paid jobs, particularly in the service sector.

Further reading

→ Artis, *pp. 315–21*
→ Beardshaw, *chapter 21*
→ Lipsey and Chrystal, *chapter 19*
→ Parkin *et al.*, *chapter 15*

Production and costs

Evaluate the extent to which the disadvantages of division of labour outweigh the advantages.

Introduction

The allocation of different jobs to different people is known as **division of labour** or **specialisation of labour**. It has taken place since society evolved beyond **subsistence level** and was first identified by Adam Smith in 1786 with his description (using the example of a pin factory) of how output can be substantially increased if the workforce specialize in particular tasks.

Main arguments or theories

Division of labour or **specialization** is very efficient compared with self-sufficiency because individual abilities differ and people can concentrate on whatever they do best. Furthermore, once someone has specialized in a particular occupation, they become better at it and can produce still more as a result—i.e. their **productivity** increases. Of course once people specialize in production of one commodity or service, they must be able to **trade** their excess production (which they do not need themselves) for the other things they need.

In a modern economy workers perform only a small part of the production process and a number of advantages result from this, such as increases in skill, time saved in moving from one task to another, and use of machinery which can perform the relatively simple subdivided operations. The resulting increase in output is considerable and makes possible **mass production**, the classic example of which is the motor-car factory production line. The disadvantages of division of labour mainly (but not exclusively) affect the workforce themselves. First, the use of machinery can result in some workers becoming **technologically unemployed**, examples being Luddites in the early nineteenth century, and printing workers in the 1980s. If a worker has a very specialized skill which is no longer required, that unemployment can be prolonged or even permanent. Secondly, specialization means that **interdependence** is increased. We depend on others for much of our needs and any disruption (such as a power-station workers' strike) can be very damaging. The third major problem with specialization is the **alienation** or estrangement which can be felt by workers if their specialized task is repetitive and boring.

Conclusion

Modern society could not exist without specialization and division of labour and the advantages of this form of production over self-sufficiency are overwhelming. There are disadvantages, but they are problems to which attention needs to be paid in order to alleviate them, rather than arguments against division of labour.

Further reading

→ Beardshaw, *chapter 3*

→ Lipsey and Chrystal, *pp. 14–17*

→ Parkin *et al., pp. 66–7*

Explain, with reference to examples, why small firms continue to exist despite economies of scale.

Introduction

It is something of a paradox that most firms are small, but most output is produced by large firms. In **manufacturing** this is particularly so, because **economies of scale** are much greater than in the **service sector**. Even in manufacturing, however, most firms are small, with under 100 employees, and the largest 5 per cent of companies produce more than 80 per cent of output.

Main arguments or theories

In industries where there are significant economies of scale, the **average cost** (*AC*) or **cost per unit of output** falls as output rises.

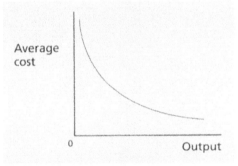

Figure 22.1 Average cost

In such a situation, large firms with higher output and lower costs per unit (such as car manufacturers or ballpoint-pen producers) can sell at lower prices than small firms. Large firms tend to dominate such industries.

Engineering provides a good example of an industry dominated by large firms but where significant numbers of small firms can still survive. These small firms may have found a small **niche market** which is relatively specialized (e.g. servicing coffee machines) in which a large firm may not consider it worth its while to compete.

Wherever the total market is small, the advantage of economies of large-scale production cannot be realized and there will be an opportunity for small firms. In this way small shops can exist to provide a relatively local service despite the lower-priced out-of-town supermarkets and hypermarkets.

In industries where scale economies are very significant the share of output of the largest few firms is considerable. Iron and steel, where British Steel produces more than 90 per cent of UK output, is a good example. In production industries where there is some element of specialism or personal service, however, the share of production of the largest few firms (the **concentration ratio**) declines; for example in brewing there are still very large numbers of small independent companies which comprise more than half of the UK market.

Conclusion

Small firms can exist even in industries where there are significant economies of scale, principally by finding a smaller, more specialized market where large firms are unlikely to compete. In those industries with the most significant scale economies such as iron and steel and motor vehicles, however, the share of output of small companies is very small.

Further reading

→ Artis, *chapter 8*
→ Beardshaw, *chapter 13*
→ Parkin *et al.*, *chapter 10*

Explain the circumstances under which a firm would continue to produce at a loss.

Introduction

In a free-market system the objective of firms is to make a **profit**. For this to happen over any particular time period, **revenue** (sales times price) must exceed costs. If costs exceed revenue then the firm is making a **loss** and it will only be able to do this for a short period of time in the expectation that things will improve (i.e. revenue will rise or costs will fall).

Main arguments or theories

In the **long run** a business which is making a loss will go out of business. In terms of costs and revenue per unit of output, average revenue (*AR*) is less than average total cost (*ATC*) and each unit produced is making a loss. Closing down immediately may not stop the losses, however, as some costs are **fixed costs** which cannot be avoided in the **short run**, e.g. cost of land and buildings or lease costs on factory and equipment.

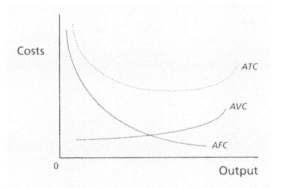

Figure 23.1 Average fixed cost, average variable cost, and average total cost

The short-run shut-down condition for the firm is in fact where *AR* (which equals price) is less than average variable cost (*AVC*), which is the direct cost of producing each unit excluding the fixed-cost element (which has already been incurred and which cannot be avoided in the short run). Examples of variable costs are labour, raw materials, and power. As long as *AVC* is covered by price, the firm can continue in business *in the short run* and if price exceeds *AVC*, then some part of the already incurred fixed costs will be paid for.

Conclusion

In the long run all costs must be covered by revenue if the firm is to remain in business. In the short run, however, the firm can continue to produce as long as average variable cost is covered by average revenue or price. In these circumstances any excess of price per unit over average variable cost will be a contribution to the fixed costs of the firm which have already been incurred and which cannot be avoided.

Further reading

→ Beardshaw, *chapter 15*

→ Lipsey and Chrystal, *chapter 11*

→ Parkin *et al.*, *chapter 10*

Why do firms seek to grow larger, and are large firms in the public interest?

Introduction

Some industries are characterized by small firms, such as retailing and hairdressing, whereas others have large firms, such as manufacturing. The cost conditions in these different industries play a large part in determining whether or not expansion of firms will lead to larger profits.

Main arguments or theories

Where there are significant economies of scale in an industry, **average costs** (cost per unit produced) will fall as output rises (see Figure 22.1). In these circumstances, large firms with a large output will be able to make the most **profit**. There are a number of different reasons for reduced costs as output increases, including: **technical economies**, **financial economies**, **administrative economies**, and **commercial economies**. Increasing the scale of production in order to take advantage of these economies of scale is a powerful motive for firms to grow larger. Where a firm produces a range of products with high development and marketing costs, there may be cost advantages in the firm being large which are known as **economies of scope**.

Firms may also seek to expand in order to gain a larger **market share**, which would increase their **monopoly power**. A greater degree of monopoly should enable greater profits to be made.

A further reason for the expansion of firms may be to avoid the possibility of takeover by another company. If the firm is large it will be more difficult for another company to raise the finance necessary for a **takeover bid**.

The question of whether large firms are in the public interest is difficult. If the reductions in costs which result from economies of scale and scope are passed on to the consumer, then the public interest is being served. If, however, the increased size of the firm gives it greater monopoly power, which can be used to reduce output and raise prices, then that is not in the public interest. It may be necessary for firms within a country to grow and increase their domestic monopoly power in order to be able to compete internationally.

Conclusion

Firms expand in order to secure cost reductions via economies of scale and of scope, and in order to increase their market share and monopoly power. Whether or not this expansion is in the public interest is a difficult decision and for this reason the **Monopolies and Mergers Commission** tends to judge each case separately on its merits.

Further reading

→ Artis, *pp. 226–34*
→ Beardshaw, *chapters 3 and 18*
→ Lipsey and Chrystal, *pp. 263–4*
→ Parkin *et al., chapter 10*

Firms

What are the main features and predictions of perfect competition?

Introduction

Perfect competition is one of the **structure–conduct–performance models** of the 'theory of the firm' in economics. A set of assumptions is made which enables a model of a perfectly competitive market to be constructed. The structure of the market determines the behaviour and performance of firms that sell in the market. In the real world fishermen and farmers often operate in perfectly competitive markets.

Main arguments or theories

The assumptions of perfect competition are:

- many buyers and many sellers
- no restrictions on entry to the industry
- products are **homogeneous** (identical)
- firms and buyers have perfect knowledge (about prices and costs in the industry)

Because of the assumptions that the firm in perfect competition will be one of many selling identical products, the firm will be a **price taker**, which means its demand curve will be horizontal (perfectly elastic) at the prevailing market price:

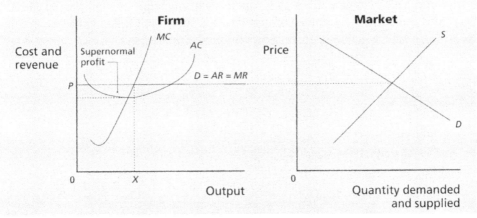

Figure 25.1 The short run in perfect competition

The diagram above shows the perfectly competitive demand curve (which is equal to the AR and MR curves) with cost conditions (AC and MC) which permit **super-normal** or **abnormal profits**. This is the short-run equilibrium diagram for a firm in perfect competition. It will only exist in the short run because of the assumption of 'freedom of entry' to the market, which will mean that new firms will be attracted into this industry, increasing supply in the market and pushing down the market price (and the individual firm's demand curve) until only **normal profits** are possible ($AC = AR$):

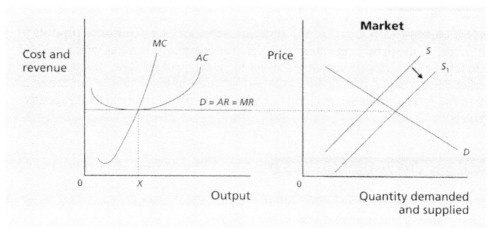

Figure 25.2 The long run in perfect competition

Conclusion

Perfect competition will be characterized by many firms selling homogeneous or identical products at prices which are dictated by the market. In the long run the main prediction of perfect competition is that only normal profits will be possible because of the entry of new firms to compete away any supernormal profits which exist in the short run. The fierce competition will also force firms to keep costs to a minimum, which makes perfect competition very **efficient**.

Further reading

→ Beardshaw, *chapter 16*

→ Lipsey and Chrystal, *chapter 12*

→ Parkin *et al.*, *chapter 11*

'Firms maximize profits where *MC* = *AC*.' Discuss.

Introduction

Explanation of **profit maximization** where $TR - TC$ is greatest, which will be where $MC = MR$ (and MC is rising).

Main arguments or theories

Show how profits are maximized in **perfect competition** where $MC = MR = AC$ using the long-run equilibrium diagram for perfect competition:

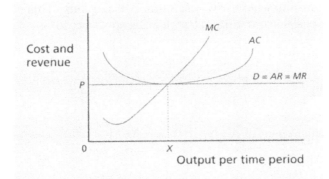

Figure 26.1 **Long-run equilibrium in perfect competition**

X is profit-maximizing output and at this output MC does equal AC, i.e. it is the **least cost** or **optimum technical output**.

In **imperfect competition**, however, profits are not maximized where $MC = AC$ but where $MC = MR$. In fact MC does not equal AC because in imperfect competition there is **excess capacity**:

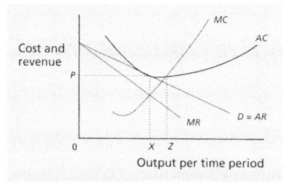

Figure 26.2 Imperfect competition in the long run

$MC = AC$ at the lowest point of average cost, which is the optimum technical output. Profits are maximized at X (where $MC = MR$) and the excess capacity is the distance $z - X$.

Conclusion

Firms maximize profits where $MC = MR$ and MC is rising. This coincides with the lowest AC in perfect competition but this is a special case.

Further reading

→ Beardshaw, *chapter 17*
→ Lipsey and Chrystal, *chapter 12*
→ Parkin *et al., chapter 13*

Discuss what you consider to be the most important limits on the size of firms in the long run.

Introduction

Explain how both small and large firms exist in many markets in the UK but certain markets seem to be characterized by small firms (give examples) while others are dominated by large firms (give examples).

Main arguments or theories

Cost conditions may determine the size of firms in an industry. **Economies of large-scale production** may occur and this will result in the market being characterized by large firms (give examples).

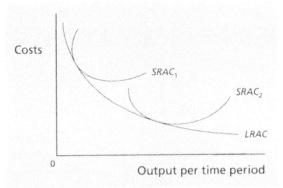

Figure 27.1 Economies of large-scale production

Where costs are constant, then both large and small firms can exist in the same market (give examples).

Where costs are increasing, then the market will be characterized by small firms (give examples).

Also, where the total market is small then there is no scope for economies of scale. This would apply to **specialized production** or to shops in small communities.

Subcontracting of small jobs by larger companies to smaller ones because there are no economies of scale in production can occur in industries such as building and engineering.

Conclusion

The size of the total market and the cost conditions which apply in a particular industry are the most important limits to the size of firms in the long run.

Further reading

→ Beardshaw, *chapter 15*
→ Lipsey and Chrystal, *chapter 11*
→ Parkin *et al., chapter 10*

What are the main features and predictions of imperfect competition?

Introduction

Explain why imperfect (or monopolistic) competition is a particularly common market form, giving real-world examples of product markets which are in imperfect competition.

Main arguments or theories

Explain assumptions of imperfect competition which define the **market structure**, i.e.

- many buyers and sellers
- differentiated products
- freedom of entry

and which dictate the **conduct of firms**. Because of these assumptions there will be

- fierce competition
- non-price competition
- only normal profits in the long run
- excess capacity (explain clearly)

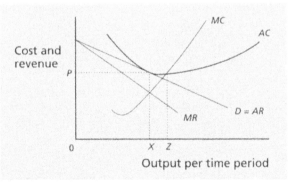

Figure 28.1 Long-run equilibrium in imperfect competition

Note that x is the profit-maximizing (equilibrium) output, where $MC = MR$ but only normal profits are possible $(AC = AR)$, and that $z - x$ is excess capacity because the profit-maximizing output does not coincide with the lowest point of the AC curve (which is the least-cost output).

Firms 73

Conclusion

Identify the main features (differentiated products and non-price competition) and predictions (normal profits and excess capacity) of imperfect competition.

Further reading

→ Beardshaw, *chapter 17*
→ Lipsey and Chrystal, *chapter 14*
→ Parkin *et al.*, *chapter 13*

'The critical assumption of the theory of the firm is barriers to entry.' Discuss.

Introduction

Brief discussion of the theory of the firm as it encompasses different market forms (**perfect competition**, **imperfect competition**, **oligopoly**, and **monopoly**). The assumption of **barriers to the entry of new firms** applies to oligopoly and monopoly but not to perfect and imperfect competition where **freedom of entry and exit** applies.

Main arguments or theories

Types of barrier to entry:

- **natural barriers**: control of raw materials; economies of scale leading to absolute cost advantages; technical reasons mean that only one firm is needed
- **barriers created by the firm**: restrictive practices such as solo marketing, predatory pricing, horizontal market-sharing
- **legal or government policy barriers**: licence or statutory right to be the sole supplier, e.g. Royal Mail; patents conferring exclusive production rights for 16 years.

The models of the theory of the firm are known as **structure–conduct–performance** models:

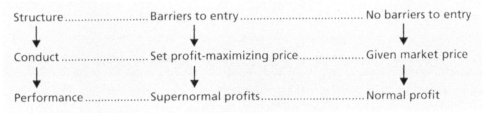

Figure 29.1 Structure–conduct–performance models

Compare monopoly (same in short run and long run) with perfect competition (short-run equilibrium different to long-run equilibrium).

Conclusion

Absence of barriers to entry leads to competition, which is efficient and removes supernormal profits.

Existence of barriers to entry enables supernormal profits in the long run.

Agree with statement in title.

Further reading

→ Beardshaw, *chapter 18*

→ Lipsey and Chrystal, *chapter 13*

→ Parkin *et al., chapters 11, 12, and 13*

Why is the behaviour of firms in oligopoly difficult to predict?

Introduction

Description of oligopolistic market structure including the following:
- few firms
- **barriers to entry**
- **interdependent actions**
- examples (banks, motor-car industry, oil industry)

Main arguments or theories

Stress importance of interdependence of actions, which means oligopolists have to 'second-guess' their rivals and adopt a **strategy**.

Four possible strategies:
1. Ignore rivals' reactions (price leaders can do this)
2. Do nothing (do not react)
3. Agree with others on a common policy (**collusion**)
4. Wait for others to lead (price followers do this)

The oligopolist may assume that
(a) a price fall *will* be matched by competitors
(b) a price rise *will not* be matched by competitors

This leads to a **kinked demand curve**:

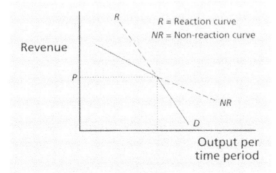

Figure 30.1 The kinked demand curve

A price cut could lead to a **price war** and there is, therefore, **uncertainty** in the market.

There is an incentive to **collude** to avoid this uncertainty.

Even then uncertainty may continue because the agreements are not legally binding (indeed they are most probably illegal) and firms may break ranks.

Conclusion

Uncertainty about competitors' reactions makes firms' behaviour difficult to predict.

This leads to many oligopoly models, each based on different reaction assumptions.

Advanced analysis of oligopoly involves **game theory**, which assesses strategies of firms.

Further reading

→ Beardshaw, *chapter 17*
→ Lipsey and Chrystal, *chapter 14*
→ Parkin *et al.*, *chapter 13*

What are the sources of monopoly, and what is the economic case for and against patents?

Explanation of the term **monopoly** involving the following:

- **sole supplier**
- **no close substitutes**
- **barriers to entry**

Main arguments or theories

Explanation of sources of monopoly, including (with relevant examples):

- control of a factor of production
- legal privileges (patents, copyright, statutes/licences)
- advantages of large-scale production (indivisibilities)
- deliberate action to exclude competitors (restrictive practices)
- product differentiation

Description of patent system using terms **temporary monopoly** and **supernormal profits**.

Arguments in favour of patents:

- stops rapid copying of inventions and allows inventors to earn profits to compensate for costs/risks of development
- provides incentives for invention and research and development
- supernormal profits may be used for product development
- may lead to consistent research

Arguments against patents:

- hinders development of other companies
- allows exploitation of customers
- monopolist can restrict supplies to raise price
- price will be greater than marginal cost

Conclusion

Patents can be a good thing for incentives to research and development but monopoly problems of restricted output and higher prices are likely to occur.

Further reading

→ Beardshaw, *chapter 18*

→ Lipsey and Chrystal, *chapter 13*

→ Parkin *et al.*, *chapter 12*

Analyse the role of the trade unions in the UK as a monopoly power.

Introduction

Explain the activities of **trade unions** including:
- acting on behalf of workers to improve pay and conditions
- their belief in strength in numbers and **collective bargaining**

In the UK, trade union membership and power declined considerably in the 1980s.

Main arguments or theories

A **pure monopoly** is a single seller of a product with no close substitutes—to some extent capital can be substituted for labour in some industries (give examples).

A **closed shop** would fulfil this monopoly criterion: only union members are allowed to work for the firm.

Generally, monopolies can increase prices by restricting output and analogy can be made:
- with **craft unions**, which restrict entry of labour by apprenticeship schemes, union cards, etc.; and with
- **industrial unions**, which aim for a closed shop within their industry.

Barriers to entry, therefore, exist in the trade union world as they do in monopolies.

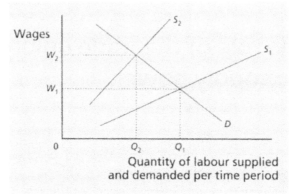

Figure 32.1 Restriction of labour supply to raise wage levels

Conclusion

In the UK, trade unions have approximately 7.3 million members, which is less than half of the workforce but sufficient to constitute a monopoly by Monopolies and Mergers Commission criteria (greater than 25 per cent).

The activities of craft and industrial trade unions have similarities with monopolistic behaviour and trade unions may act as monopoly suppliers of labour.

Further reading

→ Artis, *pp. 321–6*
→ Beardshaw, *chapter 21*
→ Lipsey and Chrystal, *chapter 19*
→ Parkin *et al.*, *chapter 15*

Compare and contrast alternative methods of dealing with monopoly.

Introduction

There is a general presumption that monopoly power is against the **public interest**—that prices will be higher and output lower than in competitive industries and that monopolies will seek to exploit consumers who have little or no choice. There may also be inefficiency in monopoly because the firm is protected from competition by **barriers to entry** and the firm may not be **X-efficient**. **Competition policy** (the laws and arrangements that exist to encourage competition and discourage monopoly) is used in the UK to influence the behaviour of individual firms and to change market structures.

Main arguments or theories

Where there is a **natural monopoly** (where **economies of scale** are so important that there is room for only one very large firm in the industry) the government may go to the extreme of taking that industry into **public ownership** as a **nationalized industry**. This was done with several industries in the post-war period, e.g. steel, gas, coal, and shipbuilding. Since 1980 many such industries have been **privatized** and their behaviour regulated by a regulatory body such as OFGAS. In this case prices are controlled so that excessive monopoly profits are not made by the company.

The Office of Fair Trading (OFT) reports to the Secretary of State for Trade and Industry in the UK. It can investigate **restrictive practices** (which attempt to reduce competition) and refer them to the Restrictive Practices Court for judgment. The OFT can also recommend to the Secretary of State that a **merger** be referred to the Monopolies and Mergers Commission (MMC). Mergers which would lead to the resulting firm having a market share which is greater than 25 per cent are thought to lead to monopoly power and are more likely to be referred to the MMC. In recent years few mergers have been referred to the MMC and fewer still have been refused. It may be, however, that the *potential* for referral to the MMC discourages dominant firms from merging to create monopolies.

Conclusion

While the ultimate method of 'dealing with' monopoly may be to take it into public ownership, very few economists would now advocate this. In fact the trend is very much in the opposite direction, to privatize and then regulate those industries where a natural monopoly exists. In the United States this policy has led to the companies 'capturing the regulators', i.e. gaining control over them so that they could act in an anti-competitive way. In the UK this has not happened thus far, although the regulatory bodies, notably OFWAT and OFTEL, have been accused of being soft in their approach.

Policies on restrictive practices and mergers have also been pragmatic and a cynical view of this was put forward by J. K. Galbraith who said that the purpose of anti-monopoly legislation is so that the government can be seen to be doing something about monopoly. It may well be that government has relaxed its controls on monopoly in order that large domestic firms can grow stronger in order to compete internationally.

Further reading

→ Artis, *pp. 245–59*
→ Beardshaw, *chapter 18*
→ Lipsey and Chrystal, *chapter 13*
→ Parkin *et al.*, *chapter 12*

How is it that sometimes two different prices can be charged for the same product or service?

Introduction

Price discrimination is a practice of producers which enables them to charge different prices for different units of the same product. They do this in order to increase profits and in doing so they take some of the consumers' surplus which would otherwise go to buyers.

Main arguments or theories

With a single price, consumers benefit because they would have been prepared to pay higher prices for some of the units purchased. This is known as **consumers' surplus**:

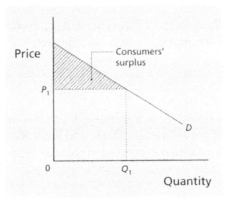

Figure 34.1 Consumers' surplus

If two or more prices can be charged to different consumers then some of the shaded area can go to the producer:

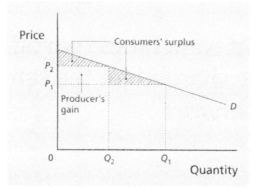

Figure 34.2 Reduction in consumers' surplus

Price discrimination is possible only if the low-price buyers cannot resell to those who face a high price. For this reason the markets in which the goods are sold must be separate (otherwise resale from one market to the other would gradually equalize prices).

Since goods are more easily resold than services, price discrimination is easier in service provision than in goods provision. Examples of services which can be sold at different prices are medical treatment (often more expensive to wealthier patients) and cinema performances (cheaper to children).

Buyers facing the high prices must have more inelastic demand than those facing low prices. Consider rail commuters into London; they have few alternatives and more inelastic demand than inter-city travellers. As a result a railway mile travelled by a commuter is more expensive than an inter-city railway mile.

Conclusion

Price discrimination by a producer is possible if there is a degree of monopoly in the markets in which the firm sells its products and if the markets can be kept separate by preventing resale among consumers. If this can be done then higher profits can be made by producers by selling at higher prices to consumers with more inelastic demand.

Further reading

→ Beardshaw, *chapter 18*
→ Lipsey and Chrystal, *chapter 13*
→ Parkin *et al.*, *chapter 12*

Discuss the economic case in favour of monopoly.

Introduction

Economic theory normally presents a powerful case *against* monopoly production on the grounds that it will lead to higher prices and lower output than competitive production. For this reason the government attempts to regulate monopolies, legislating against **restrictive practices** and encouraging competition.

Main arguments and theories

The argument that monopolies will restrict output in order to achieve higher prices overlooks the possibility that costs can be reduced by monopolised production. **Efficiency savings** could be achieved by combining a number of competing firms into an integrated unit, and larger production runs can lead to **economies of scale**:

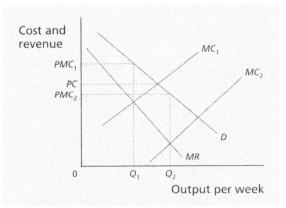

Figure 35.1 The case for monopoly

These cost savings shift the marginal cost curve to MC_2 from MC_1 leading to a price of PMC_2, which is lower than the original monopoly price PMC_1 *and* lower than the potential competition price PC. Output is also greater at Q_2.

Monopolies may also have more incentive to **innovate**, because they can reap the benefits longer relative to firms in competitive markets where there are no **barriers to entry**. More funds for **research and development** are also likely to be available to monopolies from their supernormal profits. Joseph Schumpeter argued that the benefits of innovation and economic growth which result from

Firms 87

monopoly production are much greater than any misallocation of resources which arises from monopoly exploitation.

Conclusion

There is no doubt that unrestricted monopoly power can and does lead to exploitation of consumers, via reduced output and higher prices and with consequent loss of **consumer surplus** or **welfare**. Nevertheless it can be argued that there are circumstances where monopolies operate efficiently and innovatively, with considerable economies of large-scale production which actually benefit consumers.

Further reading

→ Artis, *chapter 8*
→ Beardshaw, *chapter 18*
→ Lipsey and Chrystal, *chapter 13*
→ Parkin *et al.*, *chapter 12*

'Cartels are beneficial because they reduce uncertainty.' Discuss.

Introduction

In **oligopoly**, where there are only a few firms in the market (say 3 to 11), they can agree not to compete but to restrict output and raise prices and profits. This is known as **collusion** or a **collusive agreement** and it is illegal because it restricts competition and is thus against the interest of consumers.

Main arguments or theories

Uncertainty can be reduced if a cartel exists in a market because prices are likely to be stable and the increased profits mean that firms are not likely to go out of business. Price rigidity is a feature of an oligopolistic market:

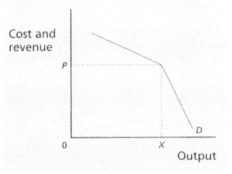

Figure 36.1 Price rigidity in oligopoly

Consider the firm's position if there is a stable price P: if it raises its price above P then other firms may not follow and so it loses a lot of sales—its demand curve above P is **elastic**; if it lowers its price below P then other firms are likely to do the same and it does not gain many sales—its demand curve below P is **inelastic**. In such a situation there is a great temptation to leave the price where it is at P.

If one or more of the firms in the cartel cheats on the agreement, however, in order to raise its own revenue, then the outcome is less certain. It may lead to a full-scale **price war** and a period of great uncertainty with some firms leaving the industry. Eventually a new collusive agreement may be made. This scenario is difficult to analyse, both for the firms, who do not know what their competitors' reactions will be to their own actions, and for economists, who use **game theory** to analyse oligopolistic markets.

The Organization of Petroleum Exporting Countries (OPEC) provides a good illustration of cartel behaviour. From 1973 to 1985 the producer countries followed the cartel agreement quite well, but successive infringements by some members eventually forced the biggest producer, Saudi Arabia, to increase its own output, causing a dramatic fall in price.

Conclusion

While cartel agreements are adhered to they can reduce uncertainty about prices and security of supply. The temptation to cheat on the agreements by one or more producers, however, means that even in relatively stable cartels there will always be uncertainty.

Further reading

→ Beardshaw, *chapter 17*
→ Lipsey and Chrystal, *chapters 13 and 14*
→ Parkin *et al.*, *chapter 13*

Market efficiency and failure

Explain the distinction between private and social costs and the problems that can result when they diverge.

Introduction

Private costs are those which are suffered by the person or firm creating them, for example the raw material costs incurred by a manufacturing company. **Social costs** are additional costs known as **externalities** or **spillover effects** which are not paid for by those people or firms who create them. Instead these costs are borne by different members of society (or society as a whole).

Main arguments or theories

Traffic congestion provides a useful illustration of the divergence between private and social costs:

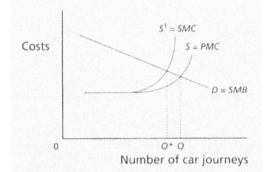

Figure 37.1 The external costs of traffic congestion

If only private costs are taken into account by motorists the volume of traffic will be Q, where **private marginal cost** (PMC) equals **social marginal benefit** (SMB). If the additional social costs of traffic congestion are taken into account, then the volume of traffic will be reduced to Q^*, where **social marginal cost** (SMC) equals **social marginal benefit** (SMB). If the extra social costs of traffic congestion are not taken into account then the volume of traffic will be greater.

Other examples of externalities include:

- factory pollution of rivers or the atmosphere
- overfishing by private trawlers

- exhaust emissions by private cars
- despoilation of the countryside by quarry companies

Conclusion

There are a variety of instances of divergence between private and social costs creating externality or spillover effects. In many cases these uncompensated costs cause problems for people who are not the originators of the costs, as in the case of pollution. In recent times the **Polluter Pays Principle** has been adopted by many governments, with the aim of 'internalizing the externality' so that those responsible for the social costs pay for them.

Further reading

→ Artis, *pp. 283–5*

→ Beardshaw, *chapter 25*

→ Lipsey and Chrystal, *chapter 24*

→ Parkin *et al., chapter 20*

Explain how a cost–benefit analysis could be done with reference to an actual or hypothetical project.

Introduction

Cost–benefit analysis (CBA) is an investment appraisal technique which began to be used in the 1960s as a method of allocating resources. It takes into account all relevant **private and social costs and benefits** (the 'wide view') and those in the distant future as well as those in the short term (the 'long view'). Social costs include private costs plus any other costs which are external to the decision-maker, for example loss of business to shopkeepers in a town where a bypass is to be built.

Main arguments or theories

CBA applies an objective set of decision-making techniques to consider whether a project justifies the resources allocated to it when all relevant costs and benefits have been evaluated. It is commonly used to appraise **public sector** projects, such as the study of the M1 motorway in 1957.

Those planners and economists conducting a CBA such as this would begin by listing all relevant costs and benefits, such as time saved by reduced journey times, increased traffic noise, lives saved (because motorways are safer than other roads), lives lost in construction accidents, etc. Values are then attached to the costs and benefits identified. Clearly this is difficult and controversial where no market exists and **shadow prices** have to be estimated by a variety of techniques which have been developed by economists over the last thirty years. Even where market prices are available they may be distorted by **taxes** and **subsidies** or **monopoly exploitation** and they must be adjusted to their genuine **factor cost (opportunity cost)**.

Where the net benefits (benefits – costs) occur some time in the future, they must be **discounted** to give a **present value** because benefits occurring at some future date are worth less than benefits received now. The choice of **discount rate** may be based on a market rate (which reflects the **opportunity cost of capital**) or a social rate (which reflects actual **social rate of time preference**).

The **Net Present Value (NPV)** of the project is found using the formula:

$$NPV = \Sigma_1^n \frac{Bt - Ct}{(1 + R)^n} - K$$

where B_t = social and private benefits arising in each year

C_t = social and private costs arising in each year

$(1 + R)$ = discount factor at rate of interest R

n = number of years over which the project has effects

$\sum_1^n$ = sum over years 1 to n

K = capital cost of project

If the *NPV* of the project is positive, then the project should proceed; if negative it should be abandoned and the resources used elsewhere (where the *NPV* is positive). In the case of the M1 study the *NPV* was positive, with a return on capital of about 7 per cent.

Conclusion

Cost–benefit analysis is a more wide-ranging technique than conventional investment appraisal because it takes a wider view of costs and benefits to enable those outside the market system (**externalities**) to be considered using shadow-pricing techniques. It is a particularly useful technique for projects in the public sector, where more normal profit and loss criteria may not be relevant.

Further reading

➔ Beardshaw, *chapter 27*

Discuss the arguments for and against cost–benefit analysis.

Introduction

Cost–benefit analysis (CBA) is used to appraise investment projects (often, but not always, in the **public sector**), taking both **private costs and benefits** and **social costs and benefits** into account. In particular it attempts to give a value to costs and benefits a long way in the future. It has been used for various projects including bridges, tunnels, airports, and motorways.

Main arguments or theories

All costs and benefits of a project will be listed and valued, including time savings, pollution, loss of view, etc. In many cases no market exists for these effects and **shadow prices** must be estimated, with the aim of showing the true costs and benefits of the project. For example, the Roskill Commission used the decrease in house prices around Gatwick Airport to estimate the **negative externality** of air-craft noise. Other techniques are less scientific and more controversial, especially where values are placed on human life.

It is usually accepted that a project can go ahead if it can realize a **potential Pareto improvement**. This means that the normal Pareto criterion of 'someone is made worse off as a result of others being made better off' is relaxed and the project can be allowed if everyone affected could, by a costless redistribution of the gains, be made better off, i.e. in principle the gainers could compensate the losers—the **Hicks–Kaldor Criterion**. Clearly this criterion can be criticized because those who are adversely affected do not actually have to be compensated and this can be regarded as unfair.

The uncertain nature of future costs and benefits also leads to criticisms of CBA. Obviously uncertainty increases with distance into the future and so projects with very long-term effects, e.g. the Channel Tunnel, have costs and benefits which are treated with some scepticism.

The choice of **discount rate** (which is used to convert future costs and benefits to **present values**) is also a controversial area. Estimated costs and benefits to future generations will be greatly affected by the choice of discount rate. A high discount rate will give a low value to benefits a long time into the future.

CBA also often involves estimates of **consumer surplus** which require very unlikely assumptions (e.g. that demand curves are linear).

Conclusion

The methods used to estimate shadow prices are the most criticized aspect of CBA. They are often considered contrived and arbitrary. Nevertheless CBA provides a procedure for evaluating investment projects which at least takes into account social effects and effects which occur a long time in the future.

Further reading

→ Beardshaw, *chapter 27*

Explain how the absence of property rights can lead to market failure.

Introduction

Property rights are legal arrangements that govern the ownership, use, and sale of property. Some resources are not exclusively owned by one person or firm, but are a **common property resource**. Fishing grounds provide a good example of common property which will tend to be overexploited because each individual fishing boat will reduce the catch to others and will not regard this as a cost because it is society's loss and not the individual's loss.

Main arguments or theories

For several types of environmental resources, well-defined property rights do not exist. This leads to a number of inefficiencies, including poor stewardship of the resource because the users do not benefit from its value as an **asset**, and **over-exploitation** because of **open access**.

Since access is open and free to the common property users, each individual will maximize his or her benefits, leading to overuse. This has been called the **tragedy of the commons** and was first identified as a problem of overgrazing on common land, leading to stock levels which were not **socially optimal**.

Because no one owns the air and the oceans, there is a tendency for firms to discharge **pollution** into the atmosphere and into the sea. The costs of this are imposed on society in general and not on the polluting firm and such costs are known as **externalities**. Since firms' costs are lower than they should be, they produce more output (and therefore more pollution) than they would if they paid the full costs of production:

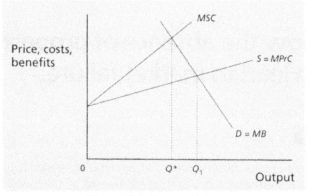

Figure 40.1 Externalities

Firms produce output Q_1 where Marginal Private Costs $MPrC$ are equal to Marginal Benefits (MB). But because of the additional costs of the externality, the Marginal Social Costs (MSC) are higher and the socially optimal output is Q^*. Because the atmosphere is a **free good**, there will be more pollution of it than is socially optimal and this is an example of market failure.

Conclusion

There are many examples of market failure which arise from an absence of property rights. Where these market failures have adverse social effects, the government may intervene to alleviate them, e.g. by setting pollution control standards. Taxation may also be used to increase firms' costs by the amount of the external cost. It may also be possible to 'internalize the externality' by using market-based environmental policies such as tradeable pollution permits.

Further reading

→ Beardshaw, *chapter 26*

→ Lipsey and Chrystal, *chapter 24*

→ Parkin *et al.*, *chapter 20*

Explain why there are inequalities in the present distribution of income and wealth in the United Kingdom.

Introduction

Income is the *flow* of earnings which a person receives, while **wealth** is the *stock* of assets which he or she owns. Incomes derive from human and non-human earnings, i.e. from work done and in the form of interest on the stock of assets held. There is considerable inequality in the distributions of income and wealth in the UK and the inequality in the distribution of wealth is greater than that of income.

Main arguments or theories

In 1989 the wealthiest 1 per cent of adults owned 18 per cent of wealth in the UK, and the wealthiest 10 per cent owned half of UK wealth. Because these assets are capable of generating income which accrues to the owner of the wealth, there is a tendency for these inequalities to continue. Moreover the poorest 50 per cent of adults owned only 7 per cent of UK wealth!

Incomes derive from assets and from human labour. Labour earns about two-thirds of total incomes. Labour incomes vary according to the individual's **marginal product**, which depends on natural ability, the level of education and skill acquired, and perhaps to some extent on luck.

Lorenz Curves can be used to illustrate the degree of inequality in income and wealth in the community, fig 41.1.

Governments can redistribute income (from rich to poor) using **transfer payments** such as retirement pensions, unemployment benefit and child benefits, and **progressive income taxes**. The UK system of taxes and benefits reduces inequality in the distribution of income but considerable inequality remains.

Conclusion

Inequality in the distribution of income and wealth exists because of differences in rates of pay and because of differences in accumulated wealth. Since wealth can generate incomes in the form of interest and dividends and since inheritance taxation is ineffective, these inequalities are likely to persist.

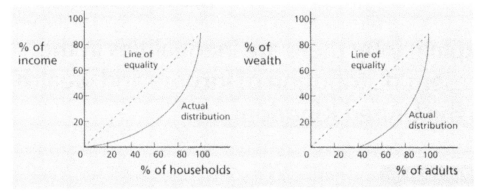

Figure 41.1 Income and wealth distribution curves

Further reading

→ Beardshaw, *pp. 382–3*
→ Lipsey and Chrystal, *chapter 24*
→ Parkin *et al., chapter 21*

Microeconomic policy

Outline the various supply-side policies which have been introduced in the UK and assess the extent to which they have influenced the performance of the economy.

Introduction

Supply-side economics emphasizes the role of **aggregate supply** in the economy, rather than **aggregate demand**. In 1803, J. B. Say claimed that 'supply will create its own demand' and this is a basic belief of supply-side economists. Policies to improve economic performance are, therefore, mainly **microeconomic policies** to improve **productivity** and supply.

Main arguments or theories

One central idea of supply-side economists is that **private enterprise** makes more efficient use of resources than the state can make of them. A key policy is reducing the state's role and enlarging that of the individual. During the 1980s and 1990s attempts to do this have included **privatization** of a number of state-run industries, including British Telecom, British Gas, and the water companies; sales of council houses to tenants at reduced prices; and attempts to reduce the **PSBR**. The first two of these have been successful in reining back the public sector, but the PSBR remains stubbornly large, mainly as a consequence of **high unemployment**.

A further main area tackled by supply-siders is policies aimed at making business and employment rewarding. These include reducing **direct taxation** to encourage work and enterprise and reducing welfare payments so that low-paid workers do not find it more lucrative to be unemployed. As a result **income taxes** have been reduced in almost every budget since 1979, with the basic rate falling from 34 to 25 per cent; and Corporation Tax (on company profits) has been reduced from 52 to 35 per cent. Welfare benefits are also more difficult to obtain. The overall burden of taxation has not fallen, however, since **indirect taxes** have been increased to make up for the lost revenue, and the effect on incentives is unclear.

Supply-siders also advocate competition and have promoted the breakup of **restrictive practices** and **deregulation of markets**, in order that free enterprise can lead to **economic growth**. Evidence as to the success of these policies is very unclear, however, because there have been two major recessions in the last sixteen years.

Finally, supply-side economics embraces a range of policies designed to improve **productivity**. These include skills training; greater overall educational standards; and reducing the power of trade unions in order to make labour more flexible. Evidence is again unclear about education and training standards, but there has been a considerable decline in trade-union influence and membership as a result of government legislation and high levels of unemployment.

Conclusion

Much of the impetus of supply-side economics has gone now that there are hardly any industries left to sell off, and there is little point in further trade-union reform since the unions are now relatively powerless. Nevertheless, it is generally accepted that the only way to reduce the **natural rate of unemployment** is through supply-side policies, although there is also acceptance that an increase in demand will be necessary to enable the UK economy to recover fully from the recession of the early 1990s.

Further reading

→ Artis, *chapter 5*
→ Beardshaw, *chapter 43*

Explain the advantages and disadvantages of the privatization of industries such as gas, water, and telecommunications.

Introduction

Public utilities in the UK such as gas, water, electricity, and telecommunications were privatized during the 1980s and 1990s. The process of privatization involves the government transferring ownership from itself (the **public sector**) to shareholders (the **private sector**). Most governments in the world embraced **free-market economics** in this period and a feature of this is less government intervention in the economy and hence the privatization of industries.

Main arguments or theories

Most UK **nationalization** (the process of the government taking ownership of important industries) took place in the period 1945–50, when it was felt that if the government controlled key industries they could be made to operate for the benefit of the country as a whole. Many of the industries which were nationalized, however, were already in **structural decline**, e.g. British Steel and British Coal, and for many years they were protected from **rationalization** (decline) by government subsidy.

Many believe that when enterprises are transferred to the private sector **efficiency** will increase because they must survive in **competitive markets** and their management must strive for high profits for shareholders. Also privatization makes it less easy for governments to use industries for political purposes, such as the reduction of unemployment.

A further reason put forward for privatization is that of **widening share ownership**. To some extent this is bound to be true although many of the initial individual subscribers to the shares tend to sell them relatively quickly to big institutional investors such as pension funds.

Privatization also raises funds for the government which can be used to invest in physical capital for the public sector or to repay outstanding government debt. It can be argued, however, that it is like 'selling the family silver' if the funds raised are used to cut taxes to finance a consumer boom.

The main argument against privatization of public utilities is that they will retain **monopoly power** which may not be used in the **public interest** if they are in the private sector. Selling off a huge industry such as British Gas as a single unit is more likely to do this than breaking up an industry into separate units, as was done with the UK electricity industry. To combat the abuse of monopoly power, various regulatory bodies have been set up which have restricted prices and forced the utilities to invest and improve their performance. Examples of such regulatory bodies are OFTEL (telecommunications), OFWAT (water), and OFGAS (gas).

Conclusion

Privatization is the result of a belief among policy-makers that markets will allocate resources more efficiently than governments. There is still a role for government to play, however, in regulating large utilities via regulatory bodies such as OFGAS, OFTEL, OFWAT, etc. Private ownership of large utilities may lead to more efficient management of rapidly changing and increasingly **capital-intensive** business, but this argument may apply to some utilities but not to others.

Further reading

→ Artis, *chapter 9*
→ Beardshaw, *chapter 19*
→ Lipsey and Chrystal, *chapter 16*
→ Parkin *et al.*, *chapter 19*

What accounts for the growth in the numbers of self-employed workers in the UK since 1980?

Introduction

Self-employed people work for themselves rather than for other employers. Until 1979 there were fewer than 2 million self-employed in the UK, but the Conservative governments of the next eighteen years made an increase in **entrepreneurship** and self-employment a key part of their **supply-side policies**, which were intended to revitalize the overall UK economy. The consequence has been a growth in the numbers of those in self-employment to more than 3 million by 1990, almost 12 per cent of the total **working population**, with income from self-employment almost 20 per cent of the total income from employment and self-employment.

Main arguments or theories

The increase in self-employment has occurred across a wide range of industries, but there have been particularly large increases in the **construction** and **service sectors**. There are several reasons for this continuing upward trend in the numbers of self-employed workers. First, the **decline in manufacturing industry** in the UK has been dramatic and jobs in that sector fell from 40 per cent in 1960 to 20 per cent by 1990. Many of the workers shed by manufacturing have turned to self-employment, often in jobs which service the manufacturing sector.

Secondly, **government policy** has actively encouraged workers to begin their own businesses, with advice and grants for new entrepreneurs.

Thirdly, many industries, local authorities, and government departments have **contracted out** jobs to small firms, often self-employed workers, rather than employing their own workers. This is particularly true of the construction industry and of cleaning and other services provided by local authorities and the health service.

Conclusion

The large rise in the numbers of self-employed workers in the UK is part of the **structural change** of British industry which has seen an increase in service-sector employment relative to manufacturing employment. Government encouragement of entrepreneurship and the tendency to contract out many of the jobs in large organizations have reinforced this trend.

Further reading

→ Artis, *chapter 10*
→ Beardshaw, *chapter 43*

Discuss the case for and against 'road pricing' in order to reduce traffic congestion.

Introduction

In the twentieth century road provision and maintenance has been paid for by the state, using revenue from taxation. This is because to some extent it is a **public good**—unless there is congestion, use of the roads is **non-rival** as it does not affect use by others. Because exclusion from roads is possible, however, the second condition of a pure public good—**non-excludability**—is not fulfilled and hence **road pricing**, or the charging of tolls for the use of roads, is possible.

Main arguments or theories

At the point where there is sufficient use of a road to cause congestion, extra traffic causes **external costs** which are not paid for by the road user. These costs include the extra pollution which occurs and time lost because journeys take longer.

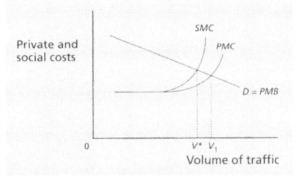

Figure 45.1 External costs of pollution

Because of these **negative externalities**, social marginal cost (SMC) is greater than private marginal cost (PMC). If only private costs are taken into account, then the volume of traffic will be V_1 where private marginal cost equals private marginal benefit. If social costs are also taken into account, however, then the optimum volume of traffic for society will be V^* where social marginal cost equals private marginal benefit. In other words, if all costs are taken into account the volume of traffic which is socially optimal is reduced.

Congestion of roads occurs because at zero price, the demand for road use exceeds the supply. Charging a price will reduce quantity demanded—some users will take another route, some will use other forms of transport or even decide not to make the journey. If the charge can be made equal to the social marginal cost of the journey, then costs can effectively be increased from PMC to SMC and the socially optimal volume of traffic can be achieved by road pricing.

The main problem with road pricing is that the cost of collection of the toll or price can be high and this is inefficient. Electronic tagging of cars is now possible, however, so that car journeys over particular pieces of road can be automatically recorded. Singapore uses the system of road pricing to good effect, ensuring that in contrast to many other cities, its traffic flows freely and pollution is reduced. In Oslo, motorists are electronically charged for peak-time use of the city's roads.

Conclusion

Road pricing provides a potential market solution to the problem of traffic congestion. Because roads are not pure public goods, i.e. they are not non-excludable, it is possible to introduce charges to reduce or eliminate congestion. The costs of such tolls can be high but improvements in technology have now reduced these costs to a minimum.

Further reading

→ Beardshaw, *chapter 25*
→ Lipsey and Chrystal, *pp. 113*

How do merit goods differ from private goods? Do these differences affect the way in which they are provided?

Introduction

Private goods such as radios, shoes, and wine have two principal characteristics: they are **rival,** which means if one person uses them then another person cannot; and **excludable**, which means that anyone not paying for them can be excluded from using them. **Public goods** are non-excludable and non-rival and include such things as national defence and street lighting. In most countries governments provide public goods. **Merit goods** are those which society deems to be especially important and which individuals should be encouraged to consume because they confer significant welfare benefits. Examples include housing, education, health care, libraries, and museums. They can be supplied by the market, however, which is what distinguishes them from public goods.

Main arguments or theories

Merit goods facilitate a **redistribution of income** because they are generally provided at less than market prices and financed by **progressive taxation**. Poorer consumers can thus take advantage of a better standard of education or health care etc. than they could otherwise afford. This has benefits for society in the form of **positive externalities** because a better-educated and healthier workforce can be good for the country as a whole.

For these reasons merit goods are often provided collectively by the state, although in the UK public and private provision of merit goods seem to co-exist in the fields of housing, education, and health with relatively little conflict.

Essentially the decision as to which goods are regarded as merit goods is a **value judgement** of society (a political decision) and for this reason there is considerable scope for disagreement over the method of provision. Free-market economists would advocate only minimum state provision either by direct state supply or by subsidy to private-sector suppliers (e.g. education voucher schemes). More interventionist economists would argue that the state should ensure adequate provision by direct supply via general taxation.

Conclusion

Although merit goods can be distributed by the price system just as private goods are, there is some justification for their provision being made on the basis of merit or need. Most governments accept this and reap the benefits of fairer income distribution and positive externalities.

Further reading

→ Beardshaw, *chapter 26*
→ Lipsey and Chrystal, *chapter 23*
→ Parkin *et al.*, *chapter 18*

Is there an economic 'North–South Divide' in the UK?

Introduction

Regional policy in Britain dates back to the 1934 Special Areas Act, which identified a number of **depressed areas** in need of assistance to promote industrial diversification. These areas were virtually all north of a line drawn from Bristol to Middlesbrough and as a result the concept of a **North–South Divide**—a poor North and a prosperous South—was born.

Main arguments or theories

In the areas of Northern Ireland, Scotland, the North, the North West, Wales, and Yorkshire and Humberside unemployment rates were significantly higher in the 1930s than in the more prosperous regions of the West Midlands, the South West, the East Midlands and the South East. The northern regions had more older 'heavy' industries such as coal mining, iron and steel, shipbuilding, and textiles which have been in decline since the 1920s, while the more southerly regions have more diverse manufacturing and service industries.

While **unemployment** levels have generally fallen, those areas that traditionally had higher rates of unemployment than the national average still have them. This suggests that **regional policy**—grants to firms which maintain or create employment—has not been a success. It is estimated that regional policy between 1960 and 1981 created 780,000 jobs but at an average cost to the taxpayer of almost £40,000. As a result regional policy expenditure has been steadily reduced from £500 million in 1984 to less than £200 million in 1996.

In the period 1971 to 1994, those areas in proximity to the South East increased their employment levels, while the main job losers were the West Midlands, the North, and the North West, where the concentration of manufacturing industries has contributed to the problem.

In Scotland, Wales, and Northern Ireland employment has increased because of **inward investment** and oil-related employment in Scotland. The recession of the early 1990s hit the economy of the South of England harder than the rest of the country. Around 1 million jobs were lost in London and the South East. Two factors account for the South being worse affected: first, the recession hit **service-sector industries** hard for the first time; and secondly the sudden **collapse of house**

prices in 1989–90 was far more pronounced in the South and the consequent loss of wealth reduced consumption, which led to job losses.

Conclusion

It is generally true that the most prosperous region of the UK is the South East. Employment and incomes are higher there than in other areas of the country, despite the setback of the early 1990s recession. The concept of a North–South Divide, however, has never been perfect, with some parts of the North remaining prosperous while parts of the South have been relatively depressed. That is certainly the case today, with Scotland in particular seeing the economic benefits of North Sea oil, and Wales, Northern Ireland, and the North East of England all seeing the benefits of inward investment.

Further reading

→ Artis, *pp. 303–5*
→ Beardshaw, *chapter 13*

Plan 48

How is competition encouraged and monopoly discouraged in the UK?

Introduction

It is widely believed that competition is beneficial to consumers and the economy as it keeps prices down and forces firms to operate efficiently. By contrast, monopolies are believed to lead to higher prices, lower output, less efficiency (and higher costs), and a **welfare loss** to society as a whole as a result of **allocative inefficiency**. As a result, since 1948 UK governments have legislated to control **monopolies and restrictive practices**.

Main arguments or theories

The **Secretary of State for Trade and Industry** oversees competition policy in the UK through the **Office of Fair Trading (OFT)**, the **Restrictive Practices Court (RPC)**, and the **Monopolies and Mergers Commission (MMC)**. Restrictive practices are anti-competitive agreements between firms which try to divide up a market in some way which reduces competition, or which try to arrange prices to reduce competition. Such restrictive practices must be demonstrated to be in the **public interest** if they are to be allowed and in order to do this they must clear one of eight **gateways** or tests. An example of one of these gateways is: 'Employment is protected by this practice.'

Monopoly and merger policy defines a monopoly as a market share of 25 per cent or more. A firm (or group of firms acting together) can be referred by the OFT and Secretary of State to the MMC for investigation if the value of the assets merged exceeds £70 million or the 25 per cent market share is exceeded.

The effectiveness of merger policy can be questioned, since less than 4 per cent of proposed mergers covered by the Fair Trading Act (1973) were referred to the MMC between 1979 and 1994 and less than half of those were declared against the public interest.

The **European Union** also has a monopoly, mergers, and restrictive practices policy to which British firms are subject if they engage in interstate trade or try to restrict trade in any way.

Another aspect of UK government policy since 1981 which has promoted competition is the **privatization** of state-owned monopolies such as British Telecom, British Gas, and British Rail and the **deregulation** of certain markets such as bus travel and road haulage. Where natural monopolies still exist after privatization they are regulated by public **regulatory authorities** such as OFWAT (water) and OFTEL (telecommunications).

Conclusion

Government policy in the UK is designed to encourage competitive practices and to discourage restrictive practices and monopolies. Restrictive-practice legislation is effective because it presumes that the action is against the public interest unless proved otherwise, whereas the opposite presumption is made about proposed mergers (where the policy is less effective). Where natural monopolies continue to exist there are regulatory bodies to deter them from abusing their market power.

Further reading

→ Artis, *chapters 8 and 9*
→ Beardshaw, *chapter 18*
→ Lipsey and Chrystal, *chapter 13*
→ Parkin *et al.*, *chapters 12 and 13*

How has the retail sector of the UK economy changed since 1960?

Introduction

Retailing is the selling of goods and services to final customers. It is a very large part of the UK economy, with more than 2.5 million employees working in more than 200,000 retail businesses. It is also a very diverse industry, with small 'corner shop' businesses and large discount stores co-existing to serve different customer requirements.

Main arguments or theories

The main trend in the structure of the retail trade in recent decades has been the **concentration of ownership** and growth in **market share** of a small number of very large companies. This is typified by food and grocery retailing, which is dominated by large companies such as Sainsbury, Asda, Morrisons, Safeway, and Tesco. The market share of these **multiple stores** has risen from 20 per cent in 1950 to 80 per cent today. Increasingly these multiples are producing their 'own brand' products, which are similar to leading brands but cheaper and with bigger profit margins.

Discount stores such as Netto are a recent development in the grocery market. They concentrate on fewer product lines and low overheads and profit margins to sell at lower prices than the multiples. While they have gained only a small market share to date, the discount stores are growing rapidly and the multiples have responded by opening their own discount stores, e.g. Sainsbury's 'Bulksava'.

In the clothing, household goods, audio-visual products, and leisure goods areas new chains of discount stores have appeared with an emphasis on price discounting. Other established companies such as Marks and Spencer and the shops in the Burton Group, which previously emphasized quality and service, have been forced to respond to low-price competition by introducing their own low-price ranges.

Warehouse price clubs have spread from the United States to sell in bulk at hugely discounted prices. They have membership schemes and aim to sell groceries and household goods quickly to reduce the amount of money which is tied up in stock.

The development and growth of large out-of-town shopping centres containing established multiple stores has inevitably contributed to the disappearance of many small retail outlets in villages and on housing estates. In addition, the comparative difficulties of parking in city centres and the preference of consumers for car journeys rather than public transport has contributed to a relative decline of town-centre shopping in many areas.

Conclusion

Retailing is a huge and enormously varied sector of the UK economy which is dynamic and continuously adapting to meet customer needs. While there has been a concentration of market share in the industry in recent times there are still many small independent retailers often concentrating on specialized goods and offering personal service and expert advice.

Further reading

→ Parkin *et al., chapter* 9

To what extent has the policy of privatization of parts of the UK public sector achieved its objectives since 1979?

Introduction

Since 1979 the UK government has sold its stake in many important industries, including motor vehicles, telecommunications, gas, coal, rail, steel, oil, and electricity. Approximately £50 billion has been raised for the Exchequer by these privatization sales and many ordinary citizens have profited from the purchase (and sale) of shares in the newly privatized companies. In addition 700,000 council houses have been sold to their occupiers.

Main arguments or theories

The first and most important stated objective of privatization is to increase the **efficiency** of the **state monopolies**, which were widely believed to be bureaucratic, inefficient, and protected from effective competition. It was believed this would be achieved by removing political control and exposing firms to the private capital market and the danger of **takeover** if they underperform. While the possibility of increased competition now exists, it has yet to appear in the **utilities** (water, gas, electricity, telecommunications), although their success in terms of profitability and efficiency gains seems clear.

The second objective, to raise **funds for government** and thus to reduce the **PSBR**, has clearly been achieved but its significance is not great in relation to overall taxation receipts. Clearly £50 billion is a huge sum of money but it has been received by the government over 16 years and at no time have privatization proceeds reduced the share of public spending in GDP by more than 1.5 per cent.

The third main objective of privatization is to **widen share ownership** to a greater proportion of the population. The proportion of adults owning shares has increased significantly—from about 7 per cent to about 23 per cent—as a result of advertising and bonus schemes. Nevertheless most shares have been bought by institutional investors and many of the individual investors sold their shares for a premium relatively quickly after purchase.

Conclusion

Whilst there has been a great deal of criticism of the way that many industries have been privatized, there is now little debate about the policy of privatization itself, and the fact that the policy has spread to governments all over the world suggests that the economic arguments for private ownership of business are sound.

Further reading

→ Artis, *chapter 9*
→ Beardshaw, *chapter 19*
→ Lipsey and Chrystal, *pp. 305–8*
→ Parkin *et al.*, *chapter 19*

Macroeconomics

Introductory Macroeconomics

Show how aggregate demand and aggregate supply can be used to illustrate and explain the level of economic activity and the price level.

Introduction

Aggregate demand is the total of all **planned expenditures** for consumption and investment, by both the private and the public sector. **Aggregate supply** is the total of **planned production** of consumer goods and investment goods.

Main arguments or theories

An aggregate demand curve AD shows total demand at various price levels. An AD curve will slope downwards to the right, meaning that there will be reduced demand at higher price levels. This is because at higher price levels, **interest rates** will be high and this will reduce demand for **consumer durables** and **investment goods**; also **imports** will be cheaper and **exports** more expensive, reducing demand for domestic goods; and finally, an increase in the price level reduces the **real wealth** of holders of cash, causing them to spend less.

The aggregate supply curve AS shows the real income or output at various price levels. At first it will be horizontal, as output can be increased without an increase in the price level because there is **excess capacity** in the economy. Approaching **full employment**, however, the AS curve will slope upwards, meaning that output increases will be accompanied by a rise in the price level.

At full employment of resources Y_F the AS curve will become vertical (see figure 51.1).

It can be seen from Figure 51.1 that an increase in aggregate demand from AD_1 to AD_2 will increase the equilibrium level of national income and output from Y_1 to Y_2 with only a small increase in the price level. Where the AS curve becomes vertical, however, any increase in aggregate demand will have no effect on output levels (with full employment of resources, output is already at a maximum level of Y_F) but will increase the price level. Increasing aggregate demand, therefore, when the economy is already working at full capacity will lead to **demand-pull inflation**.

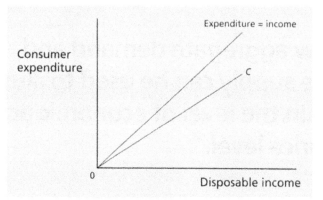

Figure 51.1 Aggregate demand and supply

Conclusion

Aggregate demand and supply curves can be used to explain how the equilibrium level of economic activity—output, employment, and incomes—is determined, and how the price level will be affected by a change in either *AD* or *AS*. In the long run the *AS* curve is vertical and an increase in national income can only be achieved by increased resources and technological advance.

Further reading

→ Beardshaw, *chapter 44*
→ Lipsey and Chrystal, *chapter 31*
→ Parkin *et al.*, *chapter 27*

Explain what is meant by 'value added' and show how it is used in calculating the national product.

Introduction

Gross domestic product (**GDP**) is the total money value of final goods and services produced in an economy in a given year. It can be calculated by three different methods: income, expenditure, or output. Each method should achieve the same final figure (although there are bound to be small statistical differences) because they are measuring the same thing at a different stage in the **circular flow of income**. So:

National income = National product = National expenditure

Main arguments or theories

To arrive at GDP using the output method, the values of output must be derived from censuses of production. Only **final output** should be included, not intermediate goods which go into final production, or **double-counting** will occur. For example, if the total output of the tyre manufacturing industry were included as well as the total output of the motor-car industry, then clearly some tyres would be counted twice, thus overestimating total output. This arises wherever the output of one firm constitutes an input or raw material for another.

To avoid double-counting, the **value added** at each stage of production must be determined—not total sales from each sector, but what has been added in value to those components bought in. In public services such as education and health the value of final goods and services is found by adding the value of all input costs such as staff wages and material costs.

The value added of various sectors is then totalled to give a figure for gross domestic product (GDP) which must be statistically adjusted to ensure it is equal to the income and expenditure measures, e.g. value added in

- agriculture, forestry, and fishing
- manufacturing
- construction
- education and health services
- ownership of dwellings

Conclusion

Each firm's value added is the value of its output minus the value of the inputs that it purchases from other firms. The sum of all values added in an economy is a measure of that economy's total output or GDP.

Further reading

→ Beardshaw, *chapter 7*
→ Lipsey and Chrystal, *chapter 28*
→ Parkin *et al., chapter 23*

Explain the concept of 'equilibrium national income'.

Introduction

When the economy is in equilibrium there is no tendency for it to change and output will neither increase nor decrease. **National income** (which equals national output) is in equilibrium when planned expenditure equals planned output. A situation where this equilibrium condition occurs can continue indefinitely. J. M. Keynes, in *The General Theory of Employment, Interest and Money* (1936), showed that this equilibrium situation has nothing to do with the employment level—the economy can be in equilibrium with significant **unemployment**.

Main arguments or theories

In a simple model of the economy with only two sectors—households and firms—equilibrium occurs where any **leakage** from the **circular flow of income** is replaced by an **injection** into the flow. Since the only leakage (or **withdrawal**) in such an economy is **saving** and the only injection is **investment**, equilibrium occurs where saving equals investment.

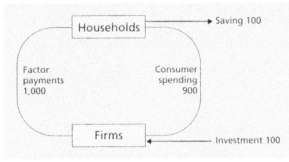

Figure 53.1 The circular flow of income

In this model the value of firms' output, which is equal to factor payments, is 1,000 and expenditure is 1,000 (consumer spending—900—plus investment spending—100).

In a more complex 'open' model of the economy with four sectors—households, firms, government, and other countries (trade)—there are more withdrawals and more injections. The withdrawals are now: saving (SA), taxation (T), and imports (M), and the injections are: investment (I), government spending (G), and exports (X). The equilibrium condition, where withdrawals equal injections, is now

$$SA + T + M = I + G + X$$

The separate components of withdrawals and injections need not be equal, just the totals. If injections temporarily exceed withdrawals, the economy will grow and a new equilibrium will eventually be established at a higher level of national income where planned injections once again equal planned withdrawals.

If withdrawals temporarily exceed injections, the economy will contract and a new equilibrium will eventually be established at a lower level of national income where planned injections once again equal planned withdrawals.

Conclusion

For an economy to be in equilibrium, the planned total of withdrawals from the circular flow of income must be equal to the planned level of total injections. This does not necessarily occur at a level of national income where there is **full employment**. In such a situation firms' output plans will coincide with consumers' expenditure plans and there will be no need for output to increase or decrease.

Further reading

→ Beardshaw, *chapter 28*
→ Lipsey and Chrystal, *chapter 29*
→ Parkin *et al.*, *chapter 23*

'Gross national product (GNP) is the best indicator of a country's standard of living.' Discuss.

Introduction

Define GNP as a measure of the total value of output of the economy in a year. It can be measured at different points in the circular flow of income as expenditure, income, or output:

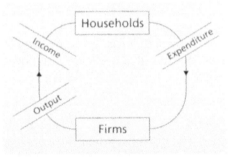

Figure 54.1 Expenditure, income, and output

Main arguments or theories

Raw GNP figures do not give an indication of living standards if they do not take account of the size of the nation's population. **GNP per head** or **per capita** is therefore a better measure for comparison.

Income distribution could be very unfair, with only a few wealthy people and the majority of the population being poor. Living standards for most of the population could be low despite high overall GNP per capita.

Gross national product does not take account of **depreciation** or **capital consumption** and Net national product (NNP) may be a better measure. NNP can be difficult to determine, however, and so GNP is often used as it is more readily available.

Climatic conditions may mean that a significant amount of expenditure on heating is necessary just to keep warm in some countries. Such expenditure boosts the GNP of that country, but is its living standard higher relative to that of a warm country?

Unrecorded transactions such as criminal activity and tax evasion will vary from country to country. In the UK the **black economy** could be as large as 10 per cent of total output.

Self-consumed produce can be significant in some economies, especially those with a large subsistence-agriculture sector.

Inflation must be taken out of the calculation of GNP if inflation rates differ between countries. Using a **GNP deflator** may not solve the problem as the choice of deflator may vary from country to country, making accurate comparison difficult.

Standard of living or **welfare** is to some extent subjective and may be influenced by many factors, among them working hours, pollution, congestion, culture, crime, etc.

Conclusion

GNP is a crude indicator of living standards. It can be used for international comparisons but for the reasons discussed above, care must be taken not to place too much reliance on its validity.

Further reading

→ Beardshaw, *chapter 7*
→ Lipsey and Chrystal, *chapter 28*

Consumption

What are the most important determinants of consumer spending?

Introduction

Consumer expenditure in the UK is the largest component of aggregate expenditure, being approximately 60 per cent of gross domestic product. Individual families with lower than average incomes, however, will tend to spend a larger proportion of their income than this, while richer families will tend to spend a smaller proportion. Plotting UK consumer expenditure against **disposable income** gives **consumption** (C):

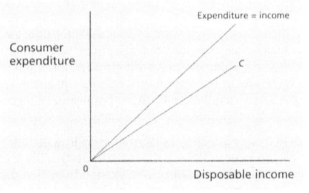

Figure 55.1 A consumption function

Main arguments or theories

Keynes's **Absolute Income Hypothesis** states that consumption is a function of income and the consumption function probably takes this form: $C = a + bY$ where a is an **autonomous** amount of consumption and bY is some percentage of income.

In these circumstances, the consumption function would look as shown in figure 55.2.

Autonomous consumption is the level of consumption when income is zero, meaning that until level of income E is reached (where expenditure equals income and savings zero) there will be **dissaving**, which consists of borrowing, stealing, or spending from savings to pay for consumption. Evidence from empirical studies would seem to support this theory.

A refinement of the Absolute Income Hypothesis was formulated by Milton Friedman as the **Permanent Income Hypothesis**. Friedman's work was based on

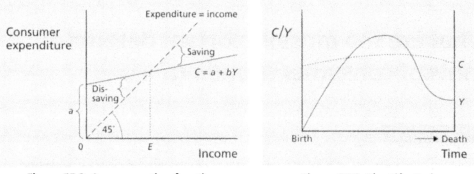

Figure 55.2 A consumption function where C = a + bY

Figure 55.3 The Life-Cycle Hypothesis

observation of the spending of US medical students, who spent more than their colleagues on other courses because they had a conception of their 'permanent income' which was higher, since they expected high earnings when they qualified. Consumption is then some function of 'permanent income': $C = f(Yp)$.

A further important theory was put forward by Modigliani, Ando, and Brumberg, who suggested that households' expenditure was influenced by 'stage of life'. Early in life, expenditure will be greater than income; then in mid-life, income will be greater than expenditure; and in retirement expenditure will again be greater than income. This theory is known as the Life-Cycle Hypothesis (see Figure 55.3).

Other, more subjective factors affecting consumer spending include: consumers' expectations (of employment or inflation), the cost and availability of credit, wealth and savings, and the conspicuous consumption of friends and neighbours.

Conclusion

Although there may be considerable short-term fluctuation in consumer spending, over the long run the major determinant of consumption at an individual level or economy-wide is income. Moreover, as incomes increase, the proportion of income which is spent falls and the proportion which is saved rises.

Further reading

→ Artis, *chapter 4*
→ Beardshaw, *chapter 29*
→ Lipsey and Chrystal, *chapter 29*
→ Parkin *et al.*, *chapter 25*

How can the relationship between consumption and income influence government policy?

Introduction

That consumption is some function of (i.e. depends upon) income is not in dispute, although the exact form of the relationship between the two may be contested. For the UK economy, consumer spending is approximately 60 per cent of national income and so the relationship could be expressed as

Consumption National Income
$$C = 0.6(Y)$$

According to Keynes's **Absolute Income Hypothesis**, the form of the consumption function is

$$C = a + bY$$

where a is some amount of **autonomous consumption** even at zero income and bY is some proportion of income. This consumption function can be illustrated as follows:

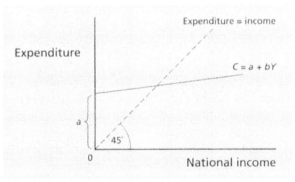

Figure 56.1 Consumption as a function of income

Main arguments or theories

It would be useful for the government to know what proportion of any increase in income is spent on consumption. This is the **marginal propensity to consume** (*MPC*) or change in consumption divided by change in income:

$$\frac{\Delta C}{\Delta Y}$$

Consumption **139**

$$MPC = \frac{\Delta C}{\Delta Y}$$

Empirical evidence suggests that the MPC is constant but that the average propensity to consume (APC) declines as income rises, which would tend to confirm the Keynesian consumption function $C = a + bY$, where b is the MPC.

An increase in income will, therefore, generate an increase in consumer spending, but the process will not end there. Because one person's spending is another person's income, a respending effect is created and any increase of income in the **circular flow** will be **multiplied** to create a still larger effect. This process is known as the **multiplier** (K) and the formula for the multiplier is given by

$$K = \frac{1}{1 - MPC} = \frac{1}{MPS + MPM + MPT}$$

Any injection into the circular flow of income will be multiplied by this respending effect, e.g. if the MPC is 0.6 then

$$K = \frac{1}{1 - MPC} = \frac{1}{1 - 0.6} = \frac{1}{0.4} = 2.5$$

which means that £100 million worth of investment injected into the economy will lead to a £250 million increase in national income. A decrease in investment would be magnified in a similar (downward) way.

Conclusion

The relationship between consumption and income provides a theoretical basis for the multiplier, which has clear policy implications for government policy since it may be possible to secure a large increase in national income (and probably employment) from a relatively modest injection of government spending or investment. It must of course be remembered that a cut in government spending or investment will be multiplied in a downward direction.

Further reading

→ Beardshaw, *chapter 30*
→ Lipsey and Chrystal, *chapter 29*
→ Parkin *et al.*, *chapter 28*

Explain the difference between consumption and investment and discuss in which category you would place education and housing.

Consumption is the act of using goods and services to satisfy **wants**, while investment is the act of producing goods that are not for immediate consumption, but are to be used to create goods and services in the future.

Main arguments or theories

Consumer expenditure takes the form of expenditure on **consumer goods**—for immediate consumption—and **consumer durables**, which provide a service over a long period of time. Expenditure on consumer durables such as washing machines is still consumption, but in everyday language confusion can be caused as people are quite likely to refer to some consumer durables as 'a good investment', meaning that they provide a service over a long period of time or that their resale value is good.

Investment is the purchase of new **plant**, **equipment**, **buildings**, and **additions to inventories**. Investment expenditure tends to be volatile, whereas consumer expenditure is a relatively stable component of national income.

Education improves and adds to labour skills and can be regarded as investment in **human capital**. Labour skills require an investment of time and resources to acquire, and they then provide increased income to their owner. A better-educated workforce is more productive and investment in education and training is an effective way of increasing national income and output.

Housing provides a stream of services over time. These services are consumed and should therefore be regarded as **current consumption**. When housing is rented then payment for these services coincides with consumption of them. When a house is purchased, however, again there can be confusion as people may well talk of 'investing in housing' or of house purchase being 'a good investment'.

Conclusion

Education can be regarded as investment in human capital with an **opportunity cost** in terms of current consumption forgone, in the same way as investment in **physical capital** requires a sacrifice of current consumption. Expenditure on housing, by contrast, should be regarded as consumption as it provides a stream of services to be consumed, albeit over a long period of time.

Further reading

→ Beardshaw, *chapter 29*

→ Lipsey and Chrystal, *chapter 29*

→ Parkin *et al.*, *chapter 25*

Saving

What are the most important determinants of saving?

Introduction

Saving is the proportion of **disposable income** which is not spent on **consumption** of goods and services. Individuals decide how much to consume and how much to save and therefore any influence on the amount spent on consumption is an influence on saving.

Main arguments or theories

The classical economists believed that consumers' expenditure and saving depended on the **real interest rate**. A high real interest rate was believed to lead to a decrease in consumers' expenditure and an increase in saving because of the reward of a higher return to compensate for giving up consumption now.

J. M. Keynes challenged this theory in his *General Theory of Employment, Interest and Money* (1936), in which he observed that people increase their consumption *as income increases*, but not by as much as their increase in income. In the 1950s the **Life-Cycle Hypothesis** (Modigliani, Ando, and Brumberg) and the **Permanent Income Hypothesis** (Friedman) suggested that consumers' expenditure and therefore saving is determined not by income but by wealth and that random fluctuations in income not associated with fluctuations in wealth will produce only small fluctuations in consumer expenditure. The **rational expectations** theories of the 1970s suggested that the average value of consumers' expenditure (and savings) will reflect long-run expectations of wealth but can be influenced by short-term changes in information and expectations about future wealth.

A number of other factors may influence people's savings, such as

1. precautionary motives—some people are more cautious than others and hence save more for any unexpected problems;
2. habits and customs—some societies may be more inclined to save than others;
3. institutional instruments which encourage saving, such as pension funds, high-interest accounts, tax-free savings plans, etc. Clearly these will vary from country to country and can be influenced by government policy;
4. inflation, which should in theory discourage saving because the money saved will be devalued, but paradoxically tends to lead to an increase in saving because it makes people uncertain about their future incomes;

5. interest rates, which do influence the amount people save, although other factors may be more important.

Conclusion

Savings are mainly deposited with financial institutions, which can then make them available to firms for **investment**. The higher the **savings ratio** (saving as a percentage of personal disposable income), the more funds will be available for investment, which can then lead to **economic growth**. The savings ratio varies from one country to another because, although income is a major determinant, saving is influenced by a variety of non-economic, cultural factors.

Further reading

→ Beardshaw, *chapter 29*

→ Lipsey and Chrystal, *chapter 29*

→ Parkin *et al., chapter 25*

Does the 'paradox of thrift' mean that saving is bad for the economy?

Introduction

Saving is a **withdrawal** from the **circular flow of income** in the sense that it is income which is received by households which is not passed back to firms as **consumption expenditure**. If **financial institutions** are able to channel the savings back into the circular flow as **investment** by firms then the flow of income is not reduced and the economy can remain in **equilibrium**.

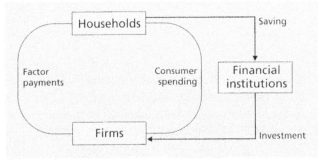

Figure 59.1 Savings and investment

Main arguments or theories

Keynes's theory of the **paradox of thrift** explains the effect of an increase in the **savings function**, which shows the proportion of income which will be saved at different levels of income.

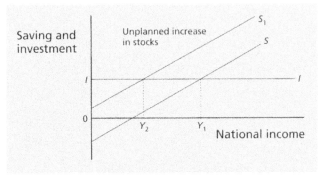

Figure 59.2 The savings function

In Figure 59.2, the savings function shifts upwards from SA to SA_I as a result of people's decisions to save more. Planned withdrawals from the circular flow exceed planned **injections** and so consumer spending must fall. Firms will find their stocks are rising and so they cut production, and after a time-lag employment will also fall. Incomes will fall and so savings will fall along SA_I (saving is a function of income) until a new equilibrium is reached at Y_2, where planned saving again equals planned investment. The paradox (unexpected result) is that the intention to save more leads to falling income and employment and therefore, eventually, to less saving.

If people are saving more because there is rising unemployment and they are fearful for the future, then increased saving will reduce real income and make the situation worse. If, however, unemployment is low then increased saving means that resources can be diverted from consumption to investment in new plant and equipment, which adds to future national income and therefore **economic growth**.

Conclusion

The paradox of thrift shows that in certain circumstances—where there is a recession and high unemployment—an increase in saving can be bad for the economy. In other circumstances, however, the extra savings can be used for productive investment, which can lead to higher rates of economic growth.

Further reading

→ Beardshaw, *chapter 28*
→ Lipsey and Chrystal, *chapter 32*
→ Parkin *et al.*, *chapter 25*

Examine the role of interest in determining saving and investment.

Introduction

Interest is the price of borrowed money or the return on money lent or saved. The **real rate of interest** equals the nominal rate minus the inflation rate. Saving is the proportion of **disposable income** which is not spent on **consumption** of goods and services. Investment is the purchase of plant, machinery, and buildings which can be used to produce goods and services in the future. Generally, a rise in the rate of interest will lead to an increase in saving and a decrease in investment, while a fall in the rate of interest will have the opposite effect.

Main arguments or theories

Say's Law and the **Loanable Funds Theory** theory suggest that saving and investment are made equal by changes in interest rates. This classical view assumed that saving and investment are equal at any level of income and so a shortfall of consumer spending due to saving would be compensated by a rise in investment. **Aggregate demand** should therefore be stable.

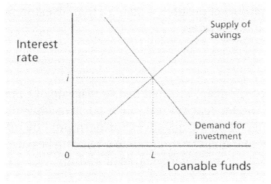

Figure 60.1 Loanable funds

Keynes showed that saving and investment decisions are made by separate groups, and a change in either is not automatically corrected by a change in the others; instead it is the resulting change in the level of income which brings them into line.

Saving will rise with the rate of interest, but it is determined by a variety of other economic and non-economic variables, the most important of which is income.

Investment will rise as the interest rate falls because the interest rate is part of the **opportunity cost** of any given investment project. The lower the rate of interest, the larger is the firm's desired capital stock:

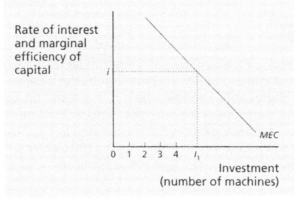

Figure 60.2 The marginal efficiency of capital

A firm will buy machines as long as the return on each—the marginal efficiency of capital (MEC) or marginal efficiency of investment (MEI) is greater than the rate of interest. In Figure 60.2, machines 1 to 4 will be purchased because their MEC is greater than the rate of interest i. Investment will be carried to the point where the MEC equals the rate of interest (at I_1).

Empirical evidence from the UK economy supports this **inverse relationship** between real interest rates and investment, although there are times, such as 1984–5, when expectations of profits are so high that investment continues to rise despite a rise in real interest rates.

Conclusion

Both saving and investment are affected by the real rate of interest. The relationship between saving and the real interest rate is positive while that between investment and the real interest rate is negative. Furthermore, the influence of interest rates is likely to be greater on investment than on saving because other influences, notably income, are important determinants of saving.

Further reading

→ Artis, *chapter 4*
→ Beardshaw, *chapter 29*
→ Lipsey and Chrystal, *chapter 29*
→ Parkin *et al.*, *chapter 25*

Investment

What are the most important determinants of investment?

Introduction

Investment is the creation of additional real capital or 'production goods' such as plant, equipment, and buildings which can be used to produce future goods and services. Investment by a firm is the amount of new capital added in a given time period. However, in any time period some capital will be used up (**capital consumption** or **depreciation**) and so

net investment = gross investment − depreciation.

Some investment is **autonomous** (explain) and some is **induced** (explain).

Main arguments or theories

The level of investment varies considerably, fluctuating between 16 and 24 per cent of GDP in the UK.

Determinants:

Interest rates
- opportunity cost of investment
- Keynesian theory of marginal efficiency of capital

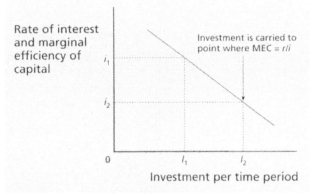

Figure 61.1 Investment and the marginal efficiency of capital

Business expectations

- whether businessmen are optimistic about the economy or pessimistic
- can be influenced by a variety of factors
- expectations can be self-fulfilling, e.g. if business managers are optimistic and they invest and then that investment itself causes an upturn

Level of national income

- a high level of national income stimulates induced investment
- the **rate of change** of national income will determine the level of new investment via the **accelerator theory** (explain)

Conclusion

Investment is very volatile and is influenced by a number of factors, the most important of which are the **real interest rate** (explain) and business managers' expectations of profits which will be influenced by where the economy is in the **trade cycle**.

Further reading

→ Artis, *pp. 44–8*
→ Beardshaw, *chapter 29*
→ Lipsey and Chrystal, *chapter 29*
→ Parkin *et al., chapter 25*

Show how consumer expenditure and investment expenditure influence the level of national income.

Introduction

Aggregate demand (*AD*) in the economy is made up of several different expenditure flows of which consumption (*C*) and investment (*I*) are two. The formula for *AD* is

$$AD = C + I + G + (X - M)$$

where *G* is government expenditure and
     (*X* − *M*) is net expenditure on exports

The level of aggregate demand is itself a key determinant of national income.

Main arguments or theories

Consumer expenditure is the amount which individuals spend on new goods and services for current consumption. Of course consumer expenditure influences the level of national income, but it is also itself a fairly stable percentage of GDP (about 50 per cent after deducting indirect taxes of 15 per cent and imports of 21 per cent in the UK). The **marginal propensity to consume** (which is the proportion of any increase in income which is spent on consumption) also determines the size of the **multiplier** (*K*), which is itself an important determinant of changes in the level of national income. The formula of the multiplier is given by the expression

$$K = \frac{1}{1 - MPC}$$

The multiplier is based on the principle that one person's expenditure is another person's income, so that an **injection** into the economy will be multiplied to give a greater final increase in national income. The process also works in reverse, so that a **withdrawal** from the economy is also multiplied to give a greater final decrease in national income.

Investment expenditure is spending by private sector businesses and the government on machines, buildings, and other **production goods** which can be used to produce future consumption goods.

Investment expenditure has a direct influence on the level of national income, as it is also part of aggregate demand. It has a longer-term influence also, as it is a major determinant of **economic growth**, which determines future levels of national income.

The **accelerator principle** describes the way in which an increase in consumer spending and hence incomes will bring about more investment and is given by the formula

$$I = a\Delta Y$$

where $a\Delta Y$ is some proportion of the change in income which will be determined by the **capital-to-output ratio**.

The increase in investment which results will itself be multiplied and lead to a further increase in national income.

Conclusion

Consumer spending and investment spending are two of the main components of demand in the economy. Consumer spending is very stable from one year to the next while investment spending tends to be more volatile. Consumer spending is likely to influence the size of the national income in the short term while investment is an important determinant in the long term.

Further reading

→ Artis, *chapter 4*
→ Beardshaw, *chapter 28*
→ Lipsey and Chrystal, *chapter 29*
→ Parkin *et al.*, *chapter 25*

Are savings and investment always equal?

Introduction

Saving is the postponement of consumption, for example by making a deposit in a bank or building society or buying an interest-bearing security. **Investment** is the process of adding to the productive capacity of the economy, for example by building a factory or purchasing new capital equipment. In macroeconomic theory actual saving always equals actual investment because of the way the terms are defined:

$Y = C + I$ (income equals consumption expenditure plus investment expenditure)

$Y = C + S$ (income equals consumption plus saving)

Therefore $C + I = C + S$ and cancelling the C on each side,

$I = S$ (investment equals saving)

In fact it is fluctuations in the volume of stocks which bring saving and investment into equality. If households planned to save more there would be a fall in consumption and stocks (which are part of investment in macroeconomic theory) would rise to bring about equilibrium between saving and investment.

Main arguments or theories

Say's Law suggests that savings could only be used for investment and that savings and investment are made equal by changes in the interest rate. There could be no excess of savings over investment (savings gap) or of investment over savings which would cause a change in aggregate demand (figure 63.1.)

J. M. Keynes identified the major determinant of household saving (and therefore consumption) as current disposable income. Investment, however, is determined by interest rates and expectations.

As a result, savings could exceed investment (or vice versa), leading to a gap in aggregate demand which could lead to low output and high unemployment. Keynes called this a **deflationary gap** figure 63.2.

Y_F is the full employment level of national income, which is not achieved because savings are in fact greater than investment and so aggregate demand is not sufficient to buy the **full employment level of output**.

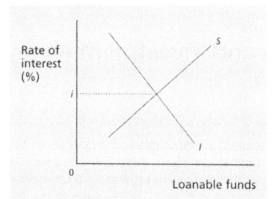

Figure 63.1 Equilibrium in the loanable funds market

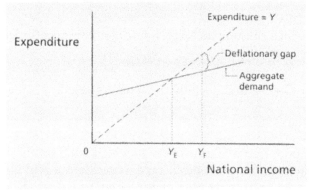

Figure 63.2 A deflationary gap

Conclusion

Because savings and investment decisions are made by separate groups, savings and investment may not be equal and this can cause fluctuations in aggregate demand, which can in turn lead to inflationary or deflationary gaps. Actual saving will be equal to actual investment but some of that actual (ex post) investment will be unplanned.

Further reading

→ Beardshaw, *chapter 29*

→ Lipsey and Chrystal, *chapters 29 and 32*

→ Parkin *et al., chapter 27*

National income determination

Explain what is meant by the 'balanced budget multiplier'.

Introduction

The **multiplier** can be defined as the ratio of the change in national income to the change in national expenditure that brought it about. It arises because of the **respending effect**: any increase in spending is respent by its recipients and respent again by the further recipients. The final change in national income is a multiple of the original increase in expenditure. A balanced budget change in government expenditure, e.g. an increase in expenditure financed by an exactly equal increase in taxation, will not have a neutral effect on national income—in fact there will be a balanced budget multiplier.

Main arguments or theories

The formula for the multiplier is

$$K = \frac{1}{1 - MPC}$$

where MPC is the **marginal propensity to consume** or spend. Since $1/1 - MPC$ is greater than one, an increase in aggregate expenditure will give a multiplied final effect on national income.

If the government increases its expenditure on goods and services by one billion pounds, which it finances by increasing taxes by one billion pounds, then national income remains unchanged only if the one billion pounds taken from the private sector is spent by that sector. If, however, the private sector saves part of the billion pounds and spends part on imported goods, while the government spends its billion entirely on domestically produced goods and services, then the balanced budget increase in government expenditure has an expansionary effect which increases national income.

Several factors complicate this analysis and modify the balanced budget multiplier effect, including inflation, the progressive nature of the tax system, and the fact that different sectors of the population have different marginal propensities to consume.

Conclusion

The balanced budget multiplier has important implications since it means that the government does not have to increase its borrowing (the **PSBR**) in order to stimulate aggregate expenditure. But because the balanced budget multiplier is relatively small compared to the multiplier for government spending alone, the size of the spending and taxation changes needed to take advantage of the effect would be large and therefore more difficult to implement.

Further reading

→ Beardshaw, *chapter 31*
→ Parkin *et al., chapter 29*

To what extent can the interaction of the multiplier and the accelerator explain the business cycle?

Introduction

Business cycles are fluctuations in **economic activity** (output, employment, and incomes) which occur irregularly in all economies (but in some more than others). Although several different types of trade cycle or business cycle have been postulated since 1945, the advanced economies have suffered business cycles lasting approximately five years.

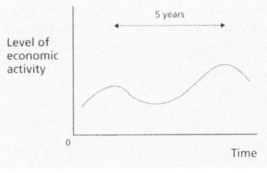

Figure 65.1 The business cycle

This pattern may have changed in recent times in the UK, with severe recessions being experienced in 1980–1 and 1991–2 and a boom period in between in 1988–9.

Main arguments or theories

There are many explanations of the causes of business cycles, including fluctuations in the **money supply, electoral cycles** as the government tries to manipulate the economy to secure re-election, **inventory** or stock adjustment **cycles**, and the theory of interaction between the accelerator and the multiplier.

The action of the multiplier is likely to reinforce any upturn (or downturn) in the economy as an increase in income is respent and therefore multiplied to give a bigger rise in national income. The value of the multiplier (K) is determined by the marginal propensity to consume (MPC) according to the formula overleaf:

$$K = \frac{I}{I - MPC}$$

The accelerator principle will also have an impact as a rise in consumption will bring about more investment. For example if the **capital-to-output** ratio is 3 to 1 then a £1 rise in consumption will bring about a £3 rise in investment. The accelerator formula is

$$I = a\Delta Y$$

where $a\Delta Y$ is some proportion of the change in income which will be determined by the capital-to-output ratio.

Moreover, the extra investment expenditure will be multiplied according to the multiplier effect. The interaction of the multiplier and accelerator will magnify a small upturn (or downturn) to create a major swing.

The theory would not be complete without explaining how the upturn could change into a downturn or vice versa, and the explanation could be provided by **interest rates**. In a boom interest rates will rise, as there will be great demand for funds. This rise in interest rates may choke off investment, leading to the end of the boom and the beginning of the downturn or recession. Similarly, in a recession there will be little demand for funds and interest rates will fall. At some point they fall so low that they trigger off an increase in borrowing for investment, which then begins an upturn or recovery.

Conclusion

Although there are many theories of the causes of business cycles it would seem that the interaction of the accelerator and multiplier, combined with the likely behaviour of interest rates, are sufficient in themselves to cause cumulative upswings and downswings in the level of economic activity and a possible explanation for the turning points.

Further reading

→ Beardshaw, *chapter 32*
→ Lipsey and Chrystal, *chapter 43*
→ Parkin *et al.*, *chapter 33*

Distinguish between the national income multiplier and the accelerator and discuss their significance for a government's macroeconomic policy.

Introduction

The **national income multiplier** is a theory which describes the multiplied effect of an increase in expenditure and shows it to be dependent on the **marginal propensity to consume** of the population. The **accelerator principle** is a theory relating the volume of **investment** to changes in national income.

The two theories are separate although they may well interact to cause upswings or downswings in the **business cycle** of the economy.

Main arguments or theories

The national income multiplier is a consequence of the **respending effect**—the fact that the spending of one group becomes income to another group, who in turn spend a proportion with yet another group. As a result an increase (decrease) in expenditure will generate a greater than proportionate increase (decrease) in income. The size of the respending is determined by the marginal propensity to consume (MPC) of the population and the formula for the multiplier (K) is given as

$$K = \frac{1}{1 - MPC}$$

The multiplier theory has obvious implications for government policy. Any increase in an **injection** into the **circular flow of income** will be multiplied according to the value of K. Also any policy which would change the value of the MPC (which will in fact vary across different income groups) would have implications for the size of the multiplier and hence for national income.

The accelerator principle describes the relationship between changes in the level of national income (GDP) and investment. According to the principle, the rate of change of income determines the level of investment and this can be expressed as

$$I = a\Delta Y$$

where I = investment

   a = some numerical value which is determined by the **capital-to-output ratio**

   Δ = change in

   Y = national income or GDP

The capital-to-output ratio may be in the region of 3 to 1 and if so a £100 million increase in demand will bring forth a £300 million increase in investment. The accelerator principle provides an explanation of why the capital goods (investment) industries are particularly susceptible to rapid upturns and downturns in trade.

The accelerator is therefore an important source of instability in the economy and if rapid upswings are to be avoided then the government must aim at a stable rate of growth of GDP.

Conclusion

The multiplier effect on national income and the accelerator effect on investment are important aspects of the economy which must be taken into account in government economic policy. They can interact, with an increase in investment being multiplied to cause a rise in national income, which in turn brings forth further investment. This process provides one explanation for the trade or business cycle.

Further reading

→ Beardshaw, *chapters 29, 30, and 31*

→ Lipsey and Chrystal, *pp. 560–3 and chapter 43*

→ Parkin *et al., chapters 25 and 28*

Evaluate the various explanations that have been put forward to explain fluctuations in the level of economic activity.

Introduction

Economists have observed that fluctuations in economic activity follow a regular pattern. A number of **trade cycles** or **business cycles** have been observed and described. A general representation of these cycles would look like this:

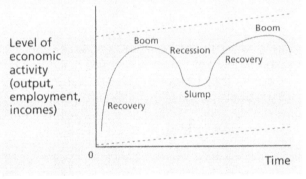

Figure 67.1 Trade or business cycles

Main arguments or theories

In the nineteenth century there appeared to be a regular cycle of booms and slumps in the UK economy, with 8 to 10 years between booms. It was felt that this was an inevitable feature of the **capitalist system**. Other observed cycles since then have been

- the **Kuznets Cycle**, which refers to a cycle of activity in building, construction, and allied industries which is of 15 to 25 years' duration.
- the **Kondratieff Cycle**, which is a long-wave cycle lasting for 50 to 60 years.
- the **Business Cycle**, which has been observed in most advanced economies since 1945, lasting 4 to 5 years.
- the **Inventory Cycle**, which is a short cycle of 1 to 2 years associated with stocking and destocking in industry.

A wide range of explanations has been put forward for the existence of trade cycles, some of them external to the economic system and some of them internal. **External theories** include the influence of wars, weather, population growth, gold discoveries, new technologies, and even sunspot activity as reasons for trade cycles. **Internal theories** concentrate on fluctuations in the money supply, technical innovations, investment patterns, and electoral influences which link trade cycles to election cycles.

For the UK in recent times, political factors seem to exert a great influence on the level of economic activity. The boom of 1988–9 and the following recession can be directly attributed to government actions and particularly manipulation of **interest rates**.

Investment changes and the interaction between the **accelerator** and the **multiplier** (investment and consumer spending) can provide a plausible reason for regular fluctuations in the level of economic activity and for **turning points** which change a boom into a recession and a recession into a recovery.

Conclusion

All economies are subject to fluctuations in economic activity and although **Keynesian demand management** policies managed to smooth out these fluctuations in the years 1945–70, they have resurfaced in the 1980s and 1990s along with the problem of **inflation**. It is likely that there are different cycles of different duration superimposed upon one another, and when their high or low points coincide the overall economy enters a boom or a recession.

Further reading

→   Beardshaw, *chapter 32*

→   Lipsey and Chrystal, *chapter 43*

→   Parkin *et al.*, *chapter 33*

What policies would you advocate to eliminate (1) an inflationary gap and (2) a deflationary gap?

Equilibrium in the economy occurs when **aggregate demand** is equal to **income**. In an **expenditure–income diagram** this is where the aggregate demand curve crosses the 45° line. If the equilibrium point coincides with the **full employment level of national income** then there will be full employment of all resources. If, however, the equilibrium occurs at any other level of income there will be an **inflationary** or **deflationary gap**:

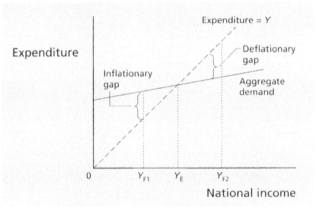

Figure 68.1 Inflationary and deflationary gaps

Main arguments or theories

An inflationary gap exists because the level of aggregate demand is greater than that which is necessary to purchase the maximum level of output (full employment level Y_{F1}) of the economy. A reduction in aggregate demand is necessary and this could be achieved using **fiscal policy** (government spending reductions or taxation increases) or **monetary policy** (measures to reduce the money supply or increase interest rates). In the early 1980s and early 1990s monetary policy was used to reduce the level of aggregate demand in the UK economy.

A deflationary gap exists because the level of aggregate demand is less than that which is necessary to purchase the maximum level of output (full employment level Y_{F2}) of the economy. An increase in aggregate demand is necessary and again this could be achieved using fiscal or monetary policy.

Keynes advocated increases in government spending (which would shift up the aggregate demand curve) in the depression of the 1930s.

It should be noted that because of the **multiplier** effect the increase (or decrease) in aggregate demand which is necessary to change national income will be less than the shortfall (or excess) of national income from the full employment level. In other words an increase in aggregate demand will be subject to a multiplier which gives a larger final increase in national income, while a decrease in aggregate demand will give a larger final decrease in national income.

Conclusion

Fiscal and/or monetary policy can be used to increase or decrease aggregate demand to remove either an inflationary or deflationary gap at a given price level. Changes in aggregate demand, however, can change both national income *and* prices and so the effects can be more complex than those predicted by the simple theory of national income determination used here.

Further reading

→ Beardshaw, *chapter 30*

→ Lipsey and Chrystal, *chapter 32*

→ Parkin *et al.*, *chapter 27*

Explain how the government can influence the level of interest rates in the economy.

Introduction

Interest is the amount paid each year on a loan, usually expressed as a percentage (or rate) of the sum borrowed.

A variety of different rates of interest will exist at any one time, each relating to different types of borrowing, but they are all related and the term **interest rate level** can be used to describe the average level of interest rates. The **Bank of England** can affect the interest rate level.

Main arguments or theories

The control of lending in the economy is achieved by altering interest rates. The Bank of England sets the rate at which it will buy or **rediscount** bills offered to it by the **discount houses** (which is known as **last-resort lending**. This sets the level of interest rates in the short-term **money markets**, which in turn determines the deposit and loan rates which the banks charge their customers. So, by forcing short-term money market rates up or down, the Bank of England can change the interest rates which banks offer to their customers.

If the Bank of England forces up short-term interest rates, the banks will raise their **base rates**, which will reduce the demand for loans. This will lead to a slow-down of economic activity and a reduction in the **money supply**. This process can be illustrated using a money demand and money supply diagram, figure 69.1.

An alternative method of influencing interest rates is by using **open-market operations**. These involve the buying or selling of government securities to firms, households, or banks, i.e. on the open market. For example, if the Bank of England wishes to lower interest rates, it will purchase securities on the open market, thus increasing the money supply (since firms, households, or the banks receive money from the Bank of England in return for their securities). Again this can be illustrated using a money demand and money supply diagram, figure 69.2.

If open-market operations are used, the change in the money supply affects the equilibrium level of interest rates.

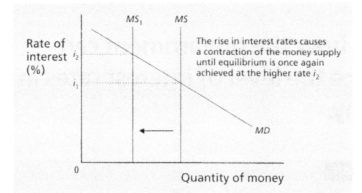

Figure 69.1 The effect of a contraction of the money supply

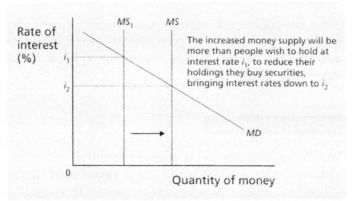

Figure 69.2 The effect of an expansion of the money supply

Since 1997, the Bank of England, independently from the government, has been able to influence interest rates and the money supply by altering its interest rate on last-resort lending and by using open-market operations. Monetary policy has been used in this way to influence the economy several times since 1979.

Further reading

→ Artis, *chapter 6*

→ Beardshaw, *chapter 23*

→ Lipsey and Chrystal, *pp. 513–15 and chapter 36*

→ Parkin *et al., chapter 31*

Money and banking

What problems are involved in measuring the supply of money in the UK?

Introduction

Money is anything which functions as a **medium of exchange**. Because of this the way in which money is defined can change over time. In the 1980s much attention was paid to **M$_1$** (notes and coin plus current account **sight deposits**) and **M$_3$** (M$_I$ plus **time deposits** with banks) but these are no longer used. Attempts to control the supply of money suffer from the problem that controls on one part of the money stock may be thwarted by expansion of a different type of money, e.g. strict controls on UK bank lending may be undone by an expansion of building society or foreign bank lending.

Main arguments or theories

Despite the tendency for different **monetary aggregates** to be targeted at different times, a general distinction can be made between **narrow money** and **broad money**. Narrow money is money which is **liquid**, i.e. immediately available for spending. In the UK this is currently **M$_0$** (the monetary base), which is notes and coin in circulation and the commercial banks' deposits of cash at the Bank of England, and **M$_2$**, which is notes and coin plus sight deposits (non-interest bearing) and **retail deposits**, which are liquid deposits of banks and building societies. Broad money includes sight and time deposits of banks plus building society deposits and **certificates of deposit** (which are traded on the money market). This is currently measured as **M$_4$** in the UK.

There are also some **assets** which are used as money in a limited way, e.g. postal orders or record and book tokens. These are **quasi-money**, while **near-money** assets are Treasury Bills and local authority bills which can be turned into cash quickly.

Since there can be some debate about exactly what constitutes money, it is obvious that measuring the money supply is bound to be a difficult task. The UK has experienced considerable difficulty in controlling the money supply since 1970 because of this difficulty of definition and because of the variety of institutions which are involved in **credit creation**. Perhaps because of this, UK monetary control has come to rely increasingly on controlling the demand for credit through **interest rates**.

Conclusion

Measuring the supply of money in the UK is a difficult problem because of the variety of assets which can perform the function of a medium of exchange. Narrow definition of the money supply is relatively straightforward and M_0 can be used as a monetary target. Broader definitions are more complex, however, and control on one type of credit can lead to diversion of borrowing to uncontrolled channels (a process known as **disintermediation**).

Further reading

→ Artis, *pp. 170–2*
→ Beardshaw, *chapter 33*
→ Lipsey and Chrystal, *chapter 35*
→ Parkin *et al., chapter 31*

Explain how and why monetary policy has changed in the UK since 1979.

Introduction

Monetary policy attempts to influence the working of the economy by changing the quantity of money in circulation and adjusting interest rates. In 1979 the UK government became strongly committed to **monetarism** in order to combat **inflation**. This led to the setting of money supply targets and the use of interest rates to help achieve those targets.

Main arguments or theories

Monetarism proposes control of the growth of the money supply in order to control inflation directly. At first the government announced **monetary targets**, particularly **sterling M3**, which consisted of notes and coins and all sterling **sight and time deposits** with the banks plus sterling **certificates of deposit**. The targets were set for four years in 1980 as the **medium-term financial strategy**.

The attempt to reduce money supply growth brought about a severe recession in the early 1980s. This was not because the targets were too strict—indeed, they were not met—but mainly because of the rise in the value of the pound which was caused by the attempt to control the money supply and the accompanying high **interest rates**.

In 1982, the government relaxed its monetary targets from 5–9 per cent to 8–12 per cent and targeted **M1** (notes and coin plus current accounts) and PSL_2 (M_3 plus building society accounts) as well as M_3.

The exchange rate crisis of 1985 finally led to the abandonment of M_3 and, while **M0** was still targeted, by the late 1980s it was clear that interest rates would be the key weapon of monetary policy.

While Britain was a member of the **Exchange Rate Mechanism (ERM)** of the European Community, between 1990 and 1992, interest rates were high in order to maintain the exchange rate at the rather high level of DM2.95. When this exchange rate became impossible to protect, Britain left the ERM and interest rates could be allowed to fall. A more pragmatic approach to monetary policy now prevails, with interest rates being used to influence the **level of economic activity** and the rate of inflation.

Conclusion

During the 1980s the UK fully embraced monetarism and announced monetary targets, and **Public Sector Borrowing Requirement (PSBR)** targets, which were designed to reduce inflation. The difficulty of keeping to these targets and the problem of a weak exchange rate gradually led to the abandonment of the medium-term financial strategy, and later to departure from the ERM. Current government monetary policy relies on the adjustment of interest rates to influence the economy.

Further reading

→ Artis, *chapter 6*

→ Beardshaw, *chapter 33*

→ Parkin *et al.*, *chapter 31*

Explain the main functions of the Bank of England and discuss the role of the Bank of England in controlling inflation.

Introduction

The **Bank of England** is the central bank of the United Kingdom. It was established in 1694 as the government's bank. By the twentieth century it had become virtually the sole issuer of bank notes and the 'bankers' bank' as it acted as banker to the commercial or **clearing banks**.

Main arguments or theories

The main functions of the Bank of England now are
- to act as the government's banker
- to act as the bankers' bank: by holding balances of the commercial banks, debts between them can be easily settled and their lending can be controlled
- to act as a **lender of last resort**: if the commercial banks get into difficulties, they can be supported by the Bank of England
- to issue bank notes
- to control or police the overall banking system
- to operate the government's monetary policy

It is mainly in this last function that the Bank of England can act to control inflation. The Bank can alter the **money supply** in several ways. First, using **open-market operations**, the Bank of England buys or sells securities (government bonds, Treasury Bills, or commercial bills) in order to change the stock of money held by the private sector. In order to reduce the money supply the Bank sells securities, which involves the lowering of the commercial banks' deposits with the Bank of England.

Another method of control which has been used by the Bank in the past is changing the required **reserve ratio** of the banks. For example, increasing the required reserve ratio reduces the size of the **money multiplier**, which restricts the banks' ability to create credit.

The same effect was achieved by calling on the banks to make **special deposits** with the Bank of England which are not part of their reserve assets.

Monetary base control, the control of 'high-powered money' which is **liquid money** held by the commercial banks with the Bank of England, has not been favoured by the authorities and instead they have principally relied on **interest rates** to control the supply of money. When the economy overheated at the end of the 1980s and inflation rose to 10 per cent per annum in 1990, the Bank of England increased interest rates (to 15 per cent in 1991) and this led to a reduction in the demand for loans, which in turn reduced consumer demand, bringing inflation under control.

Conclusion

Monetary control, which is an important determinant of inflation, is achieved in the UK by the ability of the Bank of England to determine interest rates. If interest rates are increased, there is a fall in demand for money/loans and inflationary pressure is reduced.

Further reading

→ Artis, *chapter 6*

→ Beardshaw, *chapter 35*

→ Lipsey and Chrystal, *chapter 35*

→ Parkin *et al.*, *chapter 31*

Explain how the money supply is controlled by the monetary authorities in the UK.

Introduction

The money supply is difficult to control because it is difficult to define. Anything which can perform the function of a **medium of exchange** can be considered money and this means that there is more to money than just notes and coin. The most important part of the money supply is bank deposits and the ability of the banks to **create credit** needs to be controlled by the **Bank of England**.

Main arguments or theories

In order to control bank lending, the monetary authorities/Bank of England impose a **cash ratio** or **reserve assets ratio** on banks which requires them to keep **liquid assets** as a percentage of their total assets. The higher the percentage of liquid assets which banks have to keep, the smaller is the **money multiplier**. From 1971 the banks were required to keep a 12.5 per cent reserve assets ratio. This was abolished in 1981 but the banks and other monetary institutions are still required to maintain appropriate ratios (9–12 per cent for clearing banks). An increase in the size of the ratio would bring about a large contraction in bank lending because the **money multiplier** would be reduced (money multiplier = 1/cash ratio).

Similar to an increase in the cash ratio would be a call for **special deposits**, where banks must make extra deposits with the Bank of England which they cannot count as liquid assets.

The monetary authorities can use **open-market operations** to influence the liquid assets of the banks ('high-powered money') and short-term interest rates. Open-market sales of securities (**gilts, Treasury Bills**, or **commercial bills**) can both reduce the liquid assets of the banks (because money is transferred from commercial banks to the government's account) and increase the **rate of interest** (as increased sales depress the price of securities and so increase the rate of interest which must be offered on them).

It is also necessary for the government to keep its own borrowing under control if it is to control the money supply. This is because the **Public Sector Borrowing Requirement (PSBR)** may be financed by borrowing from banks, who can use the government securities as assets to lend against.

In the early 1980s the government attempted to reduce the PSBR and adopted **monetary targets** such as **M3** and **M1** in its efforts to control the money supply and **inflation**. By the second half of the decade, however, interest rates were being used to control the demand for loans and therefore also the money supply. **Monetary tightening** involves forcing interest rates up while **monetary relaxation** means a fall in interest rates. For a brief period (1990–2) being in the **Exchange Rate Mechanism** (**ERM**) of the European Community meant that the government's ability to use interest rates as it wished was constrained by the need to meet its exchange rate commitments. Since **Black Wednesday** (16 September 1992), however, when Britain left the ERM, the government has been free to use interest rates as its main weapon to influence the level of **aggregate demand**, the money supply, and inflation in the economy.

Conclusion

The money supply can be controlled by the Bank of England in a variety of ways, which include liquidity ratios, open-market operations, special deposits, the size of the PSBR, and interest rates. Currently interest rates are the principal method of control.

Further reading

→ Artis, *chapter 6*
→ Beardshaw, *chapter 35*
→ Lipsey and Chrystal, *chapter 35*
→ Parkin *et al., chapter 31*

Why do people keep money in cash and current accounts when in other forms it can earn more interest?

There are various forms of money in a modern economy, ranging from liquid cash, which can be spent quickly, to much less **liquid assets** such as bonds. Bonds and other forms of interest-bearing wealth will be preferred to money (cash) if there is no need for liquidity. On the other hand, if money is preferred then there is an **opportunity cost** in the form of interest forgone.

Main arguments or theories

The demand for money in the form of cash exists for three reasons: for transaction purposes, for precautionary reasons, and for speculative reasons.

The **transactions motive** for holding liquid money is simply the need to pay for goods and services (because one of the functions of money is to act as a **medium of exchange**). The size of money balances held for this reason will depend mainly on the person's income and wealth, since the higher this is the more transactions are likely to take place.

The **precautionary motive** for holding liquid money relates to balances held as a contingency to cover unforeseen events and unexpected bills. Clearly the extent of precautionary balances will be affected by the psychology of the individual, but it may also be affected by the availability of credit (which makes such balances less necessary).

The **speculative motive** for holding liquid money is to avoid losses from holding bonds or securities when their price is expected to fall. A **balanced portfolio** of assets may well include some cash in case of this eventuality and in order to speculate in case interest rates should rise. Low interest rates mean that the opportunity cost of holding such speculative balances is low and so more cash might be held. If, on the other hand, interest rates are high the opportunity cost of holding liquid money is high and so liquid balances are likely to fall.

Keynes called the demand for money in the form of cash **liquidity preference** and stressed that at a time of pessimism or when interest rates were perceived to be low, people would speculate by holding money. High interest rates would then be associated with a low demand for money, while low interest rates would suggest a high demand for money. At some very low rate of interest, all wealth would be held as cash balances. This can be illustrated using a **liquidity preference curve**:

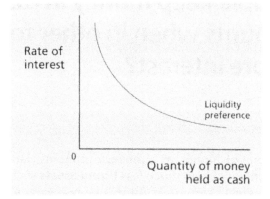

Figure 74.1 Liquidity preference curve

Conclusion

Money in the form of cash is one form of asset in the same way as other less liquid forms of wealth are assets. Fewer liquid assets give the advantage of earning interest while holding money gives the advantage of liquidity. At certain times the advantage of liquidity may outweigh the interest forgone by holding money in the form of cash.

Further reading

→ Beardshaw, *chapter 36*
→ Lipsey and Chrystal, *chapter 36*
→ Parkin *et al.*, *chapter 31*

Distinguish the money market from the capital market and evaluate the role of the capital market in the UK economy.

Introduction

Money markets are markets for short-term funds, usually less than nine months and very often overnight loans. One part of the money market is the **discount houses**, which link the **commercial banks** to the **Bank of England** and play an important role in the transmission of interest rates throughout the economy. The larger part of the money market is the **interbank market** for short-term lending between the commercial banks.

The **capital markets** are the markets for long-term finance for both industry and the **public sector**. There are many different institutions in this market, including commercial and merchant banks, insurance companies, and investment trusts.

Main arguments or theories

The capital market deals in both new issues of **securities** (equity primary shares, preference shares, and stocks or bonds) in the primary market and in existing securities in the secondary market. **Equities** are shares issued by companies and pay dividends to the holder as well as giving the possibility of a **capital gain** (or **loss**) when they are sold.

Stocks or **bonds** are interest-bearing securities. Those issued by government are **gilts** and are issued to finance the Public Sector Borrowing Requirement (PSBR), which was £23 billion in 1996. The sale of these gilts takes money from the private sector and can thus affect money supply in the economy. Stocks issued by companies are debentures which raise private sector finance, becoming redeemable at a future date and yielding a fixed rate of return. Capital gains or losses are also possible with stocks, as interest rates may vary before they mature.

Merchant banks are important to the economy because they assist companies in the issuing of new shares which raise finance for industry. Insurance companies, pension funds, investment trusts, and unit trusts all channel funds into industrial and commercial investment and as such are important to long-term economic prospects for the economy.

The secondary market, which trades existing securities, is essential to the working of the primary market because investors must be able to sell their securities for them to be regarded as liquid assets. This would normally be done on the International Stock Exchange.

Conclusion

Whereas the money market can be thought of as being essential for the day-to-day financial management of the economy, the capital market is vital for long-term development and growth and for the raising of finance for government. Some idea of how vital can be gained, however, by looking at the impact of the stock market collapse in 1987. Very little long-term damage occurred and the 'real' economy carried on working much as before.

Further reading

→ Artis, *chapter 6*
→ Beardshaw, *chapter 34*
→ Parkin *et al., chapters 30 and 31*

Public finance

Discuss how a change in the marginal rate of direct taxation might affect the level of national income.

Introduction

The **marginal rate of tax** is the tax rate which applies at the margin and as such it is very important since it is the rate which would apply to an extra unit of income. It can be expressed as

$$\text{marginal rate of tax} = \frac{\text{increase in tax paid}}{\text{increase in income}}$$

In a **progressive tax system**, the marginal rate of tax increases as incomes rise so that people with higher incomes pay proportionately more tax.

Main arguments or theories

Any increase in taxes will lead to a decrease in private sector expenditure, which is subject to the **multiplier** (which is determined by the marginal propensity to spend on domestic goods and services). If the government does not make up this reduced private sector spending with public spending, then national income could be reduced. The reverse would be true of a decrease in taxes.

The main way in which a change in the marginal rate of direct taxation would affect the economy is through its effect on **incentives**. **Supply-side** economists argue that taxes are a disincentive to effort since an increase in pay is reduced by the marginal rate of tax and this may mean that the worker does not feel that extra effort is worth while. A reduction in the marginal tax rate, it is argued, will increase incentives and lead to higher **productivity** and more output. As output increases, incomes increase, national income increases, and tax revenues actually increase. This has been the basis for the reductions in direct taxation in the UK in successive budgets since 1979. The **Laffer Curve** illustrates this possible relationship between tax rate and tax revenue—

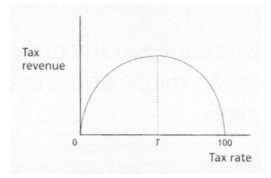

Figure 76.1 The Laffer Curve

—and suggests that there is some rate of tax T at which tax revenue will be maximized. Despite the arguments put forward by the supply-siders there is little **empirical evidence** to indicate what the rate of tax T should be; and it is very likely to vary from country to country and from time to time.

Another way in which a change in the marginal tax rate could affect national income is if the tax taken by government is **crowding out** private sector investment spending. If so, an increase in the marginal rate will lead to less private sector investment, which could reduce national income. A fall in the marginal tax rate would have the opposite effect. Of course, if the government used its increased revenue for **public sector investment** then GNP would increase.

High marginal tax rates may lead to very high income earners leaving the country as tax exiles. If high earnings correspond to high ability then this may lead to a 'brain drain', with adverse effects on technological development and innovation.

Conclusion

Supply-side economics places much emphasis on the incentive effects of a reduced marginal rate of direct taxation, but in fact there is little empirical evidence to support this view. It may even be true that an increased tax rate would lead to greater work effort in order to achieve the previous level of take-home pay (the **income effect**) instead of leading to increased leisure time because work is less rewarding (the **substitution effect**). At some point, however, a very high marginal tax rate must begin to harm incentives to work and enterprise and therefore national income.

Further reading

→ Beardshaw, *chapter 41*
→ Lipsey and Chrystal, *chapter 23*

What is the Public Sector Borrowing Requirement (PSBR)? Explain how the PSBR relates to the supply of money in the United Kingdom.

Introduction

Technically, the **Public Sector Borrowing Requirement (PSBR)** is the excess of expenditure over revenue of central government, local authorities, and public corporations minus any asset sales from **privatization**. The term is often used to refer only to the excess of government expenditure over revenue, the **budget deficit**. Since 1972 government spending has exceeded revenue each year (apart from a short period in the late 1980s) and so there has been a Public Sector Borrowing Requirement, which cumulatively adds to the **national debt**.

Main arguments or theories

UK governments have consistently found it difficult to balance the budget and at times they have deliberately used **deficit financing** as a tool of **fiscal policy**. **Keynesian economists** believed that the most important effect of the PSBR was its impact on the overall level of economic activity, whereas **monetarists** argued that the PSBR has damaging **inflationary effects** over the long term.

In fact the inflationary impact of the PSBR depends on *how* the deficit is financed. This can be done in four ways:

- by issuing more cash to the public ('printing money')
- by borrowing from overseas or in foreign currency
- by selling financial assets such as Treasury Bills to the **commercial banks**
- by selling debt (national savings, government bonds, etc.) to the non-bank private sector.

Only the last of these methods will not directly increase the **money supply**, because in order to buy the government securities, the non-bank sector, i.e. households and firms, must give up cash. If a bank acquires government securities, however, these can be used as **liquid assets** to expand the money supply by an increase in bank lending.

Clearly the first two methods of financing the PSBR will directly increase the domestic money supply.

Offsetting the inflationary effect of an increase in the money supply, however, may be an increase in **interest rates**, which restricts the demand for borrowing in the economy. This may happen because of the **crowding-out effect**—the government is in effect in competition with other borrowers of funds, and an increase in government borrowing may force up the level of domestic interest rates.

Conclusion

The PSBR is the annual budget deficit of the UK government. Unless it is financed exclusively by sales of government financial assets to the non-bank sector, it will increase the domestic money supply, which in turn is likely to increase the **rate of inflation**.

Further reading

→ Artis, *chapter 7*
→ Beardshaw, *chapter 41*
→ Lipsey and Chrystal, *chapter 42*
→ Parkin *et al.*, *chapter 29*

How might the government use fiscal policy to influence the economy?

Introduction

Fiscal policy is the use of government expenditure and taxation to influence the level of **aggregate expenditure** and the performance of the economy. It is used in conjunction with **monetary policy** and **direct intervention** to try to achieve the government's objectives of full employment, stable prices, economic growth, a satisfactory balance of payments position, and redistribution of income.

Main arguments or theories

Government expenditure (G) is one of the components of **aggregate demand**, the others being consumption (C), investment (I), and net exports (exports X minus imports M):

aggregate demand $= C + I + G + (X - M)$

If the level of aggregate demand is insufficient to purchase **full-employment output** (Y_F), then a **deflationary gap** exists:

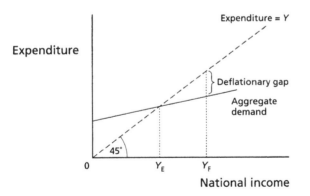

Figure 78.1 The deflationary gap and national income

The economy is in equilibrium at Y_E, where aggregate demand equals output, but there is unemployment because demand is insufficient to purchase Y_F, the level of output produced at full employment. It may be possible for the government to increase aggregate demand by increasing government spending, which would shift the aggregate demand curve upwards and close the deflationary gap. A similar effect could be achieved by reducing taxation with the aim of increasing consumer spending (C).

If aggregate demand is greater than that which is necessary to purchase full-employment output, then an inflationary gap exists:

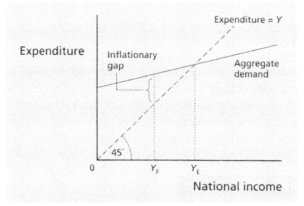

Figure 78.2 The inflationary gap and national income

In this situation, the excess demand will lead to inflation. To remove the problem the government could reduce government spending or increase taxation (reducing consumption) in order to shift the aggregate demand curve downwards.

Conclusion

The government can use fiscal policy in pursuit of its macroeconomic objectives and during the period 1945–70 it was used effectively. Government spending can cause **crowding out** of private sector investment, however, and increases in taxation may lead to **disincentives** to work and enterprise. Fiscal policy may take longer to implement than monetary policy because of the complicated legislative process which must be observed when large changes in government spending or taxation are being considered.

Further reading

→ Artis, *chapter 7*
→ Beardshaw, *chapter 41*
→ Lipsey and Chrystal, *pp. 580–3 and 619–25*
→ Parkin *et al.*, *chapter 29*

Discuss the view that the government ought to aim to balance its budget.

Introduction

Every autumn the Chancellor of the Exchequer announces the government's taxation and spending plans for the next twelve months. When taxes exceed spending there is a **budget surplus** (and the circular flow of income is reduced, which is **deflationary**). When spending exceeds taxes there is a **budget deficit** (and the circular flow of income is increased, which is **reflationary**).

Main arguments or theories

Government spending and taxation will be influenced by the level of national income. In a recession, tax receipts fall as incomes fall, and government spending rises (as unemployment rises). In a boom, tax receipts rise and government spending falls.

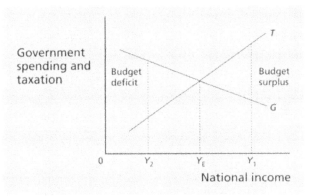

Figure 79.1 Budget deficits and surpluses

To some extent government taxation and spending compensate for lack of activity in the economy in a recession (and over-activity in a boom), acting as **automatic stabilisers** for the economy.

The major problem with a budget deficit or **Public Sector Borrowing Requirement** is that an increase in government purchases of goods and services can lead to increased interest rates and a consequent **crowding out** of private sector investment.

Also, if the government finances its borrowing in such a way that it causes the money supply to rise (by the sale of bonds to the Bank of England, which results in the creation of additional money) then higher aggregate demand will result, which eventually leads to a higher price level (**inflation**).

One further problem with government borrowing is that the interest payments on the **national debt** (which is the cumulative public sector borrowing requirements for each year) may be a constraint on future government spending if they become too large. Currently the national debt is about 40 per cent of GDP and interest on it is £4.8 billion.

Conclusion

Ideally, the government should aim to cover its spending with its income and balance its budget. Between 1972 and 1996, however, there were 21 years of budget deficits and only 3 years (in the late 1980s) of budget surpluses. Economic circumstances may mean that the government must use expansionary fiscal policy, which results in government borrowing.

Further reading

→ Artis, *chapter 7*
→ Beardshaw, *chapter 41*
→ Lipsey and Chrystal, *chapter 42*
→ Parkin *et al.*, *chapter 29*

Inflation

Plan 80

Examine the difficulties which can arise in trying to measure the cost of living.

Various measures of the cost of living are used in the United Kingdom, including the **Consumer Expenditure Deflator** (**CED**), which is based on the **national income accounts**, the **Taxes and Prices Index** (**TPI**), which was introduced by the government in 1979 in order to take account of reductions in direct taxation, and the **Retail Prices Index** (**RPI**), which is the most widely used measure.

Main arguments or theories

Changes in prices of goods and services will change the cost of living for households. In order to measure the price level, a **price index** is constructed which attaches more importance or **weight** to those goods and services which are most important in the 'average' household budget. A major problem lies in the selection of the representative basket of goods and services, and by representing the average consumer, clearly changes in the cost of living for every consumer will not be accurately measured. Rich and poor consumers will be affected in different ways—for example a rise in air fares may affect one group but not another.

Once the representative basket of goods has been chosen, and appropriate weights have been attached to each item in order to reflect their relative importance, the basket is measured at **base-year prices**, which are then expressed as 100. The basket is then revalued and reweighted to give a measure of current-year prices in relation to 100, e.g. if the new index is 103.5 then the **rate of inflation** or rise in the cost of living between the two years is 3.5 per cent.

Clearly the task of collecting the information on general prices is a major difficulty; more than 130,000 prices are checked by Department of Employment officials on the third Tuesday of each month.

A further major difficulty in measurement of the cost of living over time is caused by the fact that household expenditure patterns change over time. For example, spending on leisure services has become significant in recent times, but was not considered before the 1980s.

The Retail Price Index does not show changes in the **quality of goods** or changes in taxes and benefits which can affect **living standards**.

Conclusion

Attempting to measure the cost of living using an index of general prices conceals changes by averaging across households. Particular price changes which affect some households more than others may be disguised by this averaging process. Nevertheless, the Retail Prices Index is widely accepted in the UK as the best measure of the cost of living available.

Further reading

→ Artis, *chapter 4*
→ Beardshaw, *chapter 33*
→ Lipsey and Chrystal, *pp. 509–11 and 522–4*
→ Parkin *et al.*, *chapter 23*

Discuss the proposition that inflation is the single most important economic problem.

Introduction

Inflation is a rise in the general level of prices and therefore a fall in the value of money. Since 1975 control of inflation has been the main objective of government policy in the UK, often at the expense of other macroeconomic objectives, notably employment.

Main arguments or theories

There are four important aims of government economic policy: **full employment** (or reduced unemployment), **economic growth**, a reasonable **balance of payments** position, and **stable prices** (or low inflation). Which of these is considered the most important problem may well depend on the circumstances of the time. For example, in the 1930s the record levels of unemployment were undoubtedly regarded as the biggest economic problem and in the 1950s, balance of payments problems were dominant.

There may also be **trade-offs** between these economic policy aims. For example, pursuit of economic growth may cause the economy to 'overheat', leading to inflation. And policies to reduce inflation have adverse consequences for employment.

The government's attention to the problem of inflation stems from the belief that the other economic objectives cannot be tackled effectively unless inflation is first brought under control. Inflation has the effect of increasing **uncertainty**, which makes economic planning difficult for households, firms, and government. It discourages **saving** (because the value of money falls) and discourages **investment** (because nominal rates of interest will be high). Inflation also makes **exports** more expensive and **imports** cheaper and is therefore likely to have an adverse effect on the balance of payments.

The relationship between inflation and **unemployment** is complex and thought to be inverse, i.e. if inflation is high, unemployment will be low and vice versa (the **Phillips Curve** relationship). It is certainly true, however, that policies adopted in the UK to reduce the rate of inflation—deflating the economy by increasing interest rates—have led to increased unemployment.

Conclusion

Low levels of inflation, of 2 or 3 per cent, are not regarded as being a big economic problem; indeed they may even be helpful to business by stimulating profits. Higher rates of inflation, however, are likely to be extremely damaging and de-stabilizing to an economy. Uncertainty and adverse effects on investment and a flight of capital to lower-inflation economies are likely to be very damaging. For these reasons, control of inflation is widely regarded as a prerequisite for economic prosperity.

Further reading

→ Artis, *chapter 4*

→ Beardshaw, *chapter 42*

→ Lipsey and Chrystal, *chapter 40*

→ Parkin *et al.*, *chapter 32*

Why have UK governments found it difficult to control inflation?

Introduction

In the 1950s and 1960s inflation was very low in the UK, averaging about 3 per cent. In the 1970s, however, inflation rose dramatically, reaching 25 per cent in 1975. In 1979–81 and 1988–90 inflation rates again rose (to 22 per cent and 10 per cent respectively) and although inflation has fallen to around 2 per cent in the mid-1990s, many fear that it will return when the **level of economic activity** increases.

Main arguments or theories

Inflation can be caused in different ways, although **monetarists** would argue that it is 'always and everywhere a monetary phenomenon'. There are three main theories of the causes of inflation. The first is that it is caused by a supply shock which increases costs, leading to **cost-push inflation**. The supply shock could be in the form of a high level of pay settlements or a large rise in the price of an imported raw material (e.g. the OPEC oil price rise in 1973).

The second theory is that inflation is caused by excessive demand, leading to **demand-pull inflation**. This could result from easing of restrictions on credit.

Monetarists believe that the cause of inflation is simply an increase in the money supply—if the **velocity of circulation** is constant and in the short run output is constant, then according to the **Quantity Theory of Money**,

$MV = PT$,

where M = money supply,
$\quad V$ = velocity of circulation,
$\quad P$ = price level, and
$\quad T$ = output or volume of transactions,

if M rises then P must rise and so an increase in the money supply leads to an increase in the price level (inflation).

Once inflation begins to increase it can be **self-fuelling**—

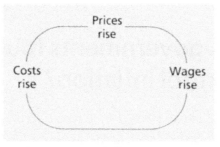

Costs rise → Prices rise → Wages rise

Figure 82.1 An inflationary spiral

—and this kind of **inflationary spiral** can be hard to break. If workers and producers expect a rise in prices then they will build this expectation into their wage claims and pricing plans and the expectation becomes self-fulfilling.

Since 1970, whenever the UK economy has experienced increased economic growth it has been accompanied by upward pressure on the price level. Successive governments have been forced to put a brake on the economy by increasing interest rates in order to reduce the rate of inflation. A 'boom and bust' pattern seems to have emerged, with the booms coinciding with increases in the inflation rate and being followed by recessions which coincide with reductions in the inflation rate.

Conclusion

It seems that the UK economy finds it difficult to experience **sustained economic growth** without an increase in the rate of inflation. The increased demand and wage pressure which accompanies rising employment, output, and incomes triggers off inflationary pressures which are hard to control other than by **deflation of the economy** using the monetary weapon of high interest rates.

Further reading

→ Artis, *chapter 4*
→ Beardshaw, *chapter 42*
→ Lipsey and Chrystal, *chapter 40*
→ Parkin *et al.*, *chapter 32*

Assess the significance of the Natural Rate of Unemployment Hypothesis for the conduct of economic policy.

Introduction

UK economic policy from 1945 to 1970 used **demand management** to solve any problems of increasing unemployment. A rise in unemployment would be met by an expansion of demand via monetary or fiscal policy. It was thought that the economic problems of unemployment and inflation could not co-exist. The **Phillips Curve Hypothesis** (1962) appeared to confirm this. High rates of unemployment *and* inflation in the 1970s led to a fundamental revision of economic theory which included the **Natural Rate of Unemployment Hypothesis**.

Main arguments or theories

The natural rate of unemployment is a key part of the **monetarists'** view of the economy. It is the unemployment which remains when the labour market is in equilibrium.

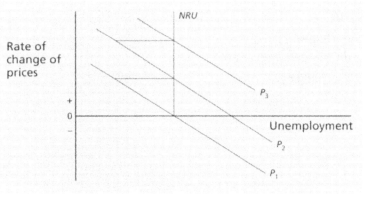

Figure 83.1 The natural rate of unemployment

Attempts to reduce employment below its natural rate—say along Phillips Curve P_I in Figure 83.1—using expansionary fiscal or monetary policy result in a temporary reduction in unemployment and an increase in the rate of inflation. As workers and other economic agents build the higher rate of inflation into their wage claims and expectations, unemployment goes back to the natural rate NRU but with a higher level of inflation. Attempting to reduce unemployment via demand management simply leads to higher levels of inflation.

Since the natural rate of unemployment could not be reduced by demand management, attention turned to **supply-side policies** to reduce it. These include

- policies to reduce **frictions in the labour market** such as:
      curbs on the powers of trade unions
      training/retraining to improve occupational mobility
      housing policies to improve geographical mobility
      reductions in unemployment benefit
- policies to create jobs through competition (and privatization)
- policies to create incentives to work by restructuring taxes
- investment in education to improve the quality of the workforce

Conclusion

The realization that unemployment and inflation (**stagflation**) could exist at the same time led to a fundamental reappraisal of economic policies in the 1970s. The acceptance by many economists of the Natural Rate of Unemployment Hypothesis has since led to successive governments relying on supply-side policies to reduce unemployment.

Further reading

→ Artis, *pp. 116–17*
→ Beardshaw, *chapter 43*
→ Lipsey and Chrystal, *chapter 41*
→ Parkin *et al., chapter 32*

Discuss how a government's commitment to stable prices is likely to affect the level of unemployment.

Introduction

After the Second World War, unemployment was low for more than twenty years in the UK. The government was committed to **full employment** and, following **demand management** policies, managed to keep unemployment below 1 million. During the 1960s and particularly the 1970s, however, the **rate of inflation** began to rise, making it much more difficult for the government to stimulate demand in order to reduce unemployment as this would add to inflationary pressures.

Main arguments or theories

Inflation and unemployment are negatively related and **empirical evidence** from the UK economy over long periods of time seems to confirm this. The **Phillips Curve** relates the level of unemployment to the rate of change of money wage rates (which are a proxy for inflation).

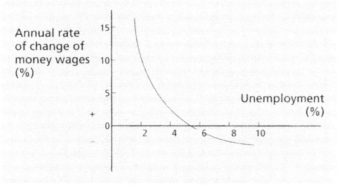

Figure 84.1 The Phillips Curve

This relationship appeared to have broken down in the 1970s, with high levels of unemployment and high rates of inflation occurring at the same time (known as **stagflation**). **Monetarist economists**, however, put forward the explanation that in an inflationary world the Phillips Curve would shift upwards by the expected rate of inflation. In other words unemployment needs to be higher if inflation is to be stabilized—there is a 'natural rate' or **NAIRU (non-accelerating inflation rate of unemployment)** at which prices will be stable.

The last three major increases in inflation in 1972–5, 1979–81, and 1988–90 have been followed by increases in unemployment as higher interest rates and a **monetary squeeze** have caused recessions. Successive UK governments have accepted that stable prices are an economic priority which must be addressed before attention can be turned to **economic growth** and consequent reductions in unemployment.

Conclusion

Although the experience of concurrent high inflation and high unemployment during the 1970s cast doubts on the Phillips Curve trade-off between inflation and unemployment, most economists and politicians now accept that a rise in inflation must be avoided or mitigated by a monetary squeeze. This reliance on the weapon of interest rates to control the economy means that a rise in unemployment is likely to be the consequence of any future rise in inflation.

Further reading

→   Artis, *pp. 110–11*

→   Beardshaw, *chapter 42*

→   Lipsey and Chrystal, *chapter 40*

→   Parkin *et al., chapter 32*

Unemployment

Evaluate different economic explanations of the current level of unemployment in the United Kingdom.

Introduction

In the UK **unemployment** is defined as the percentage of the workforce out of work but seeking employment and registered for state benefits. The percentage in mid-1997 was 8 per cent and falling, which is about 2 million of the workforce of 27 million.

Main arguments or theories

Even when there is **full employment** there will still be an unemployment rate of approximately 2 per cent because there will always be people between jobs. Some people quit their jobs and others enter the workforce taking time to find a job. This is **frictional unemployment**.

Structural unemployment occurs because the economy is constantly changing, with some industries expanding and taking on workers and others contracting and laying off workers. Very often the workers from the declining industries do not have the skills required by the expanding industries—a **skills mismatch**.

Seasonal unemployment occurs in occupations which are tourist- or weather-related, such as those in the hotel and construction industries. Because of this type of unemployment, the unemployment statistics are **seasonally adjusted** in order to analyse long-term trends.

Technological unemployment can occur when new technology replaces jobs and skills such as typesetting in the printing industry. **Demand-deficient unemployment**, or **cyclical unemployment** (so called because it varies with the trade cycle), occurs when the total demand in the economy, **aggregate demand**, is insufficient to purchase all of the goods and services produced, **aggregate supply**.

The unemployment which exists when the economy is at **potential GDP** is the **natural rate of unemployment**. This is a controversial topic, with **monetarist** economists arguing that it is the level of unemployment which is consistent with equilibrium in the labour market, and that it cannot be reduced by increasing aggregate demand.

A refinement of this idea is the **non-accelerating inflation rate of unemployment** or **NAIRU**, which is the theory that there is a level of unemployment which is compatible with stable inflation. The relationship between inflation and unemployment is complex and involves consideration of the **Phillips Curve**, but suffice it to say that the last two recessions in the UK have seen inflation fall and unemployment rise.

Conclusion

The current level of unemployment in the UK is a composite of different types of unemployment. Of the total of 8 per cent of the workforce unemployed, some 2 per cent are likely to be frictionally unemployed, while of the remaining 6 per cent a significant number are unemployed due to deficient demand (which can be expected to improve as the recovery gathers momentum). Others are structurally unemployed, particularly in the older industrial regions, where the coal, steel, shipbuilding, and textile industries have declined.

Further reading

→ Artis, *chapter 10*
→ Beardshaw, *pp. 672–4*
→ Lipsey and Chrystal, *chapter 41*
→ Parkin *et al.*, *chapter 32*

What are the various factors which determine the level of aggregate output and employment?

Introduction

The level of output or **gross domestic product (GDP)** and the level of employment are closely related. Any expansion of output is likely to lead to an expansion of demand for labour. And a rise in unemployment (without a significant increase in **productivity**) is likely to be accompanied by a fall in GDP. Both output and employment are therefore affected by the same influences on the macroeconomy.

Main arguments or theories

Neo-classical economists believed that general unemployment could only be a temporary problem caused by market frictions and that a fall in wages was all that was necessary to solve the problem. **Say's Law** (1803) held that supply created its own demand because one person's spending is another person's income, and the economy would self-regulate. Keynes, however, in his *General Theory of Employment, Interest and Money* (1936) showed that the economy could be in **equilibrium** at less than **full employment**. Keynes's central proposition was that the level of real GDP is determined by **aggregate demand**.

In Figure 86.1 the aggregate supply curve *AS* is horizontal and if aggregate demand increases from AD_1 to AD_2 then real GDP increases from Y_1 to Y_2.

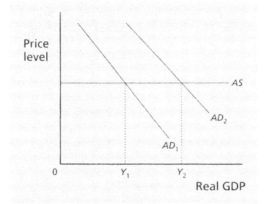

Figure 86.1 The effect of an increase in aggregate demand with a horizontal aggregate supply curve

Modern macroeconomics puts forward the possibility that there is a **natural rate of unemployment** in an economy which corresponds to **potential national income**, and is associated with **stable inflation**. In this view the aggregate supply curve becomes vertical, meaning that successive increases in aggregate demand would eventually have no effect on output, but would merely serve to increase the price level:

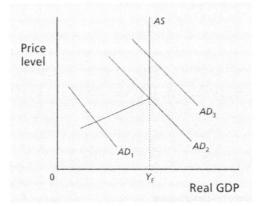

Figure 86.2 The effect of an increase in aggregate demand with a vertical aggregate supply curve

Y_F is the **full-employment level of national output**. Long-run aggregate supply may be less than Y_F because there is a natural rate of unemployment.

Conclusion

Output and employment are determined by the interaction of aggregate demand and aggregate supply in the economy. While Keynes showed how it was possible for governments to achieve full employment by adjusting aggregate demand using **fiscal policy** and **monetary policy**, the increase in inflation rates in the 1970s and 1980s has led governments to turn their attention to **supply-side economics** in their attempts to reduce the natural rate of unemployment.

Further reading

→ Beardshaw, *chapter 44*
→ Lipsey and Chrystal, *chapter 27*
→ Parkin *et al.*, *chapter 27*

Discuss whether or not it is possible to reduce unemployment without increasing inflation.

Introduction

Inflation is a rise in the general level of prices and a fall in the **value of money**, while **unemployment** is the number of workers who are not employed and who are seeking jobs. It might seem at first that there could be little relationship between the two; but in fact there is strong **empirical evidence** to suggest that they are **inversely** or **negatively related**.

Main arguments or theories

In 1962 Professor A. W. Phillips put forward the theory that high unemployment was associated with low inflation and vice versa:

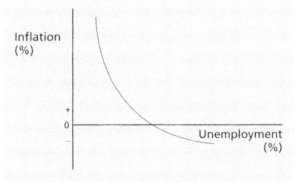

Figure 87.1 The Phillips Curve relationship

Phillips's data covered the period 1862–1958 and his theory seemed to hold until the 1970s, when inflation rose to unprecedented levels (25 per cent in 1975) and unemployment rose too (to 1.5 million in 1976). It was argued by Milton Friedman, the famous **monetarist**, that the Phillips Curve had shifted to the right because when workers and employers expect inflation, they build that expectation into their actions. As a result the Phillips Curve would shift upwards by the expected rate of inflation and the level of unemployment needed to stabilize prices—the **natural rate of unemployment** (or **non-accelerating inflation rate**, **NAIRU**) would be higher. The negative relationship between unemployment and inflation seems to have reasserted itself in the 1980s and 1990s, with UK governments even admitting that unemployment was 'a price worth paying' (Norman Lamont, 1992) in order to bring inflation down.

Keynesian remedies for unemployment—to stimulate aggregate demand using fiscal or monetary policy—did not seem appropriate in the light of Phillips theory and attention has turned in recent years to the use of supply-side policies to reduce the natural rate. These policies include

- trade union reforms to make the labour market more flexible
- reductions in unemployment benefits to discourage **voluntary unemployment**
- reductions in direct taxation to give **incentives** to work
- **privatization** to stimulate free-enterprise growth
- **deregulation** of financial services and other areas to encourage investment
- education and training to make workers more employable

Conclusion

The last three major periods of inflation (1972–5, 1979–81, and 1988–90) have been followed by recessions which have led to large increases in unemployment. Supply-side policies are an attempt to bring down the level of unemployment without adding to inflation. It remains to be seen whether the unemployment of the early 1990s recession can be significantly reduced without an increase in the rate of inflation.

Further reading

→ Artis, *chapter 4*
→ Beardshaw, *chapter 42*
→ Lipsey and Chrystal, *chapter 40*
→ Parkin *et al.*, *chapter 32*

Evaluate the economic costs which result from unemployment in the UK.

Introduction

Very low levels of unemployment or **full employment** existed in the UK between 1945 and 1970. In the 1970s the unemployment level rose to more than 1 million and in the recession of the early 1980s it rose to more than 3 million. Although the boom of the late 1980s reduced that figure to 1.6 million, it quickly rose to more than 3 million again in the early 1990s recession. Slow recovery has brought this down to just under 2 million.

Main arguments or theories

Unemployment on this scale—8 per cent of the **working population** in mid-1997—has considerable costs. The first and most obvious is the cost of unemployment and other benefits, which are a considerable proportion of **public spending**. A further impact on the public finances comes in the form of **taxes** not paid by those out of work. Although many of those unemployed would have been relatively low-paid and therefore have paid only small amounts of tax, the total sum is still significant. A reasonable estimate of the benefit-plus-tax impact is that each unemployed worker costs the government an average of £9,000 per year. With 3 million unemployed this would cost the Exchequer £27 billion per year. Costs of this size severely hamper government policy and expenditure plans.

Once unemployed, some workers, particularly those approaching retirement age, drop out of the workforce altogether. Their skills are lost to the economy and skill shortages can lead to reduced rates of **economic growth**. In this way, prolonged unemployment can cause deterioration of **human capital**.

To an economist, however, by far the greatest cost of unemployment is the true **opportunity cost**, which is the output of goods and services which are not produced by those out of work. Every day of unemployment represents lost production which can never be regained. The value of that lost production considerably reduces GNP and thus has a detrimental effect on living standards.

More indirect costs can also be the result of prolonged periods of unemployment, such as increased crime rates, psychological problems for those unemployed, and increased homelessness.

Conclusion

The costs of unemployment to the UK economy are considerable and long-lasting. The immediate costs in terms of benefits and lost taxation are significant in themselves but they are greatly exceeded by the long-term costs of lost output, lost earnings, and reduced GNP, which can never be recovered.

Further reading

→ Artis, *chapter 10*

→ Beardshaw, *chapter 43*

→ Lipsey and Chrystal, *chapter 41*

→ Parkin *et al.*, *chapter 24*

What is meant by the term 'mobility of labour'? Would increasing the mobility of labour reduce unemployment, and if so, how?

Introduction

There are two main types of mobility of labour: **occupational mobility** and **geographical mobility**. Occupational mobility is the ability of workers to move from one type of job to another, while geographical mobility is the ability of workers to move from a job in one area to the same kind of job in another area.

Main arguments or theories

Occupational mobility of labour is important to an economy in order that **structural change** can take place in its industries without large-scale unemployment occurring. If the coal-mining sector declines, then it is beneficial if workers are able to move into jobs in other expanding parts of the economy, such as the service sector. This type of mobility is enhanced if the workforce is highly educated and trained with transferrable skills. It is also helpful if there are few restrictions on entering occupations imposed by unions.

Geographical mobility of labour is important if there are regional differences in employment opportunities, a situation which has tended to persist in the UK, with better employment prospects in the South East and the Midlands than in other areas. Workers may be reluctant to move to another area because of family and other local ties, because of the problem of renting or buying a house in a more prosperous area, because of educational differences, and because of the financial cost of moving.

Even in times of high unemployment in the UK **skill shortages** exist in certain industries and anything which increases the general skill and training level of the workforce will improve this and reduce unemployment. Assistance by firms or government with relocation will also enable workers to move to another area in order to take a job.

In the UK a particular problem is encountered in the housing market because there is a relatively small private rental sector compared to other developed countries. In most areas there are waiting lists for council housing and there are large price differentials between houses in the more prosperous regions and those with high levels of unemployment.

Conclusion

Immobility of labour, either geographical or occupational, can mean higher levels of unemployment persist for longer periods than they would otherwise. Policies to increase mobility of labour, particularly better education and training and more widely available rented accommodation, would reduce the numbers unemployed and the length of time for which they remain unemployed.

Further reading

→ Beardshaw, *chapter 21*
→ Lipsey and Chrystal, *chapter 18*
→ Parkin *et al., chapter 24*

International trade

What are the advantages of international trade? Are there any disadvantages?

Introduction

International trade takes place because there are gains to be made from **specialized production** and because differences in **productive efficiency** between countries means that there will be cost differences and price differences, which leads to a pattern of trade developing.   *comparative advantage*

Main arguments or theories

In the modern world no country is self-sufficient. The basis of international trade is **specialization and exchange**. Different countries have different natural resources and factors of production and this leads to differences in production costs. Countries supply goods to the world economy which they can produce cheaply; and they buy goods which other countries can produce more cheaply. That all countries can benefit from this **free trade** is an important principle called **comparative advantage**.

There is an obvious advantage in trading when it is done in order to obtain goods which cannot be produced very easily in your own country, e.g. bananas and coffee in Britain.

Even if one country does not have a clear or **absolute advantage** in the production of any commodity, it can still benefit from trade by specializing in what it is *relatively* best at producing. Countries do import goods which they could produce for themselves and some of these goods they could produce more efficiently than the countries from which they are importing. David Ricardo (1772–1823) illustrated this principle of comparative advantage with reference to trade in wine and cloth between England and Portugal:

Labour hours per unit of output		
	Cloth	Wine
Portugal	90	80
England	100	120

Figure 90.1 Comparative advantage

Even though Portugal has an **absolute cost advantage** in the production of both commodities it would still be to Portugal's benefit to produce only wine and exchange for cloth. It would benefit England to concentrate solely upon the production of cloth, where its **comparative cost disadvantage** is least (10 to 9, whereas for wine it is much greater, 12 to 8). Ricardo showed that if a unit of English cloth is exchanged for a unit of Portuguese wine, both countries gain. England gains by 20 hours because it takes 120 hours to produce the wine in England but only 100 hours to produce the cloth. Portugal gains 10 hours by trading wine for cloth because it only takes 80 hours to produce the wine as opposed to 90 to produce the cloth.

Many disadvantages are, however, claimed to arise from free international trade, which lead some economists and politicians to call for **protectionism**. Among them are claims that trade will lead to

- **unemployment**, as imports replace domestically produced goods
- difficulties for new or **infant** industries
- **strategic problems** of over-reliance on imported supplies, e.g. oil and food
- unfair competition from subsidized or **cheap-labour** goods.

Conclusion

Countries have different factor endowments and different tastes. This means that there will always be potential gains from trade. Increased specialization should lead to greater output and further gains from trade. Britain's history seems to confirm this: the gradual removal of all protective customs duties in Britain between the 1820s and the 1870s was accompanied by an enormous expansion of trade and industry. There may be problems for particular industries in individual countries as they adjust to foreign competition but the Uruguay Round of the **General Agreement on Tariffs and Trade (GATT)** (now the **World Trade Organization, WTO**), which further reduced trade restrictions in 1994, was believed to be worth $200 billion to the world economy.

Further reading

→ Beardshaw, *chapter 37*
→ Lipsey and Chrystal, *chapter 25*
→ Parkin *et al., chapter 3*

Discuss the likely consequences of a fall in the exchange rate for the balance of payments and the rate of inflation.

Introduction

The **exchange rate** is the rate or price at which two national currencies exchange for each other, often expressed as the amount of foreign currency which can be bought using a unit of domestic currency. For example, for most of 1996, one pound was equal to approximately 1.53 US dollars.

Main arguments or theories

With a **fixed exchange rate** system, the currency can be **devalued**, i.e. a new lower rate is set for it by the government or central bank. With a **floating exchange rate** system, which has generally applied in the UK since 1972, market forces can lower the value of the currency if its supply exceeds the demand for it on the foreign exchanges. This is described as **depreciation**.

The UK did have a brief period of two years (1990–2) in the **Exchange Rate Mechanism (ERM)** of the European Community. During this time the rate was fixed within a range of 6 per cent. When the UK left the ERM in September 1992, the pound fell significantly (by 11 per cent during September and October).

When the exchange rate falls, the domestic price of foreign goods (imports) rises, depressing the demand for them. Exports, however, will fall in price or be more profitable. For these reasons the balance of payments position may improve, but only if the **elasticities of demand** for imports and exports are relatively high (the **Marshall–Lerner condition**).

It may be that a devaluation improves the **current account** of the balance of payments but only after a time-lag. This is because volumes of exports and imports take time to adjust to the change in their relative prices. Contracts for imports will already have been made and orders for more of the now cheaper exports will take time to come through. This is known as the **J-curve effect of devaluation** and is shown in the following diagram:

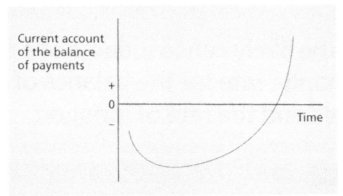

Figure 91.1 The J-curve effect of devaluation

Inflation is likely to be increased by a fall in the exchange rate because import prices will go up. This can cause **cost-push inflation** because so many raw materials used in the UK are imported. Only if the devaluation/depreciation leads to such a large rise in export volumes that economic growth increases markedly are inflationary pressures likely to be lessened.

Conclusion

A fall in the exchange rate can improve the current account of the balance of payments if the elasticities of demand for exports and imports are favourable. If they are relatively inelastic, however, then the current account will worsen. Furthermore, having to pay more for imports means that devaluation/depreciation is likely to add to inflationary pressures.

Further reading

→ Artis, *chapter 11*
→ Beardshaw, *chapter 39*
→ Lipsey and Chrystal, *chapter 37*
→ Parkin *et al.*, *chapter 36*

Explain what is meant by the 'terms of trade'. What might cause these to move in a country's favour?

Introduction

The **terms of trade** is a measure of the relative prices of **imports** and **exports** which is expressed as the ratio of the average price of a country's exports to the average price of its imports, with those goods which are most important in trade **weighted** accordingly. The **terms of trade index** shows the quantity of exports which must be given up in order to buy a unit of imports.

Main arguments and theories

The terms of trade can be calculated using the formula

$$\text{terms of trade index} = \frac{\text{index of export prices}}{\text{index of import prices}} \times 100$$

Since the terms on which one country exchanges its exports for imports are measured by prices, any influence on those prices will alter the terms of trade. Prices can change because of change in the ratio of costs of production (e.g. a rise in wage costs in one country relative to another), or because of a change in the **exchange rate** of a country.

For the terms of trade to move in a country's favour, its export prices must rise relative to its import prices; the index will then rise. Demand for the country's exports must be **inelastic**, however, in order that the rise in prices does not result in too large a fall in export volumes.

If the index falls, import prices have risen faster than export prices and the terms of trade are said to have worsened, although again elasticity of demand, this time for imports, will decide whether the country's trading position worsens or improves.

If the terms of trade consistently improve, i.e. the index rises over a period of time, the most likely explanation is that the currency of the country has risen relative to other currencies, probably because of consistent **trade surpluses**. This was the experience in West Germany and Japan in the 1970s and 1980s. Since fewer exports have to be given up to gain a given volume of imports, average **living standards** will increase in such countries.

Conclusion

The terms of trade measures the relative prices of imports and exports of a country and they are said to improve when the index of export prices rises relative to the index of import prices. The most likely explanation for this over a period of time is a rise in the exchange rate of the country, which is the result of economic and trading success.

Further reading

→ Beardshaw, *chapter 38*
→ Lipsey and Chrystal, *p. 469*
→ Parkin *et al.*, *chapter 36*

Discuss whether or not the formation of trading blocs such as the European Union contributes to an increase in economic welfare.

Introduction

The EEC or Common Market, now the **European Union (EU)**, was established by the Treaty of Rome in 1957, although the UK did not join until 1972. Its main features are: the removal of **tariff and quota barriers** between member countries; European-wide standards for goods; the removal of border controls between members; and ultimately **monetary union**, which will mean a single European currency.

Main arguments or theories

A **common market** or **trading bloc** exists when goods and services are freely tradeable within the **customs union** area but common tariffs and quotas are imposed on goods and services coming from outside the area. Since any restriction on trade is likely to lead to an overall loss of production for the world economy, the European Union or another trading bloc such as the North America Free Trade Area (NAFTA) could be seen as reducing overall economic welfare. This is because **free trade** will allow regional specialization and increased world production.

Trade within the European Union is increased, however, because of the efficiency gains created by the removal of restrictions. This must be offset by the extent of **trade diversion** to more expensive sources of imports as a result of the **Common External Tariff**. An example of such trade diversion for the UK is butter, which before 1973 could be purchased from New Zealand at world prices. After 1973 it came from more expensive European sources. The impression of the EU being a **protectionist** organization has been created mainly by the **Common Agricultural Policy (CAP)**, which has imposed major import restrictions which were defended during the Uruguay Round of the **General Agreement on Tariffs and Trade (GATT)** so that trade in agricultural goods is still restricted.

Since 1992 the abolition of restrictions on movement of capital (**exchange controls**) has led to the creation of a single market in financial services.

The removal of trade barriers within the European Union may lead to welfare gains based on the principle of **comparative advantage**, i.e. increased output, employment, and incomes from specialization and increased production. There will also be welfare losses from **unemployment** in UK industries which cannot compete effectively with those in other European countries.

Conclusion

The creation of a European single market has liberalized trade within the EU and has not led to significantly reduced trade with the rest of the world except in agricultural products. The gains to European firms, which are able to take advantage of significant **economies of scale** in a market of more than 300 million people, are considerable and may well outweigh any welfare loss from the Common External Tariff.

Further reading

→ Artis, *chapter 3*
→ Beardshaw, *chapter 40*
→ Lipsey and Chrystal, *chapter 26*

Exchange rates

Taking into account recent experience, critically assess the view that 'allowing the pound to float' is better for the United Kingdom than a fixed exchange rate.

Introduction

The **exchange rate** of the UK is the price at which the pound can be traded for another currency. In the longer term it is determined by **demand for UK exports** and our **demand for imports** from other countries. In the short term there can be considerable fluctuation caused by **currency speculation**, interest rates, and good or bad economic news.

Main arguments or theories

With a **fixed exchange rate**, the value of the pound is maintained at (or close to) a certain value against other major currencies. The Bank of England intervenes in the foreign exchange market—by using its reserves of foreign currencies to buy sterling if there is downward pressure on the pound—or by selling sterling if there is upward pressure on the pound.

With a **floating exchange rate**, the value of the pound is determined by its demand and supply in the **foreign exchange market** without intervention by the Bank of England. From 1972 to 1990 the pound was allowed to float on the foreign exchanges. This had the advantage that any disequilibrium in the **balance of payments** could be automatically rectified by a change in the exchange rate without the necessity for the government to use **deflationary policy** (leading to unemployment and lower growth).

In 1990 the UK joined the **Exchange Rate Mechanism (ERM)** of the European Community. The ERM is neither a fixed nor a floating rate, although the currencies of the countries in the system are fixed against each other while the whole currency bloc can fluctuate against currencies from other parts of the world, such as the dollar. The pound was allowed to fluctuate within a 6 per cent band of its central rate of DM2.95 (most other EC countries were fixed within a narrower band of 2¼ per cent). By 1992 the pound had become the weakest currency in the system and was constantly near the floor of its wider band (DM2.80). This necessitated Bank of England intervention, either by buying pounds using foreign currency reserves, or by raising domestic interest rates, which would attract inward investment (necessitating purchase of pounds by foreign investors). Finally on 16 September 1992 the pressure was too great and the government was forced to admit defeat and leave the ERM. Since then the pound has floated and settled nearer a free-market rate of DM2.25.

Leaving the ERM coincided with the beginning of the **recovery** in the UK—possibly because the lower exchange rate led to increased demand for exports (which became cheaper) and reduced demand for imports (which became more expensive). The fall in the value of the pound certainly indicates that the pound was overvalued within the ERM.

Conclusion

The UK has a weak balance of payments position, which makes adhering to a fixed exchange rate system (even one with some flexibility like the ERM) very difficult. Trying to defend the currency can lead to interest rates which are higher than they would otherwise be, which can lead to recession. On the other hand, exporters and importers prefer the stability of fixed exchange rates, which makes their planning and pricing more certain.

Further reading

→ Beardshaw, *chapter 39*
→ Lipsey and Chrystal, *pp. 761–2*
→ Parkin *et al.*, *chapter 36*

How does membership of the Exchange Rate Mechanism of the European Monetary System affect a government's ability to pursue an independent monetary policy?

Introduction

The **European Monetary System** was founded in 1979 to try to prevent competitive devaluations among **European Union** countries and to reduce the risks and uncertainty of inter-country trade. The UK joined the ERM later in 1990 but left chaotically on 16 September 1992, which became known as **Black Wednesday**.

Main arguments or theories

Essentially, membership of the **Exchange Rate Mechanism** (**ERM**) means operating a virtually **fixed exchange rate** system. If the value of the currency is fixed (albeit within a narrow band of 2¼ per cent or the broader ERM band of 6 per cent of its value) then upward or downward pressure on it must be tempered by government action. A fall in the demand for UK exports, for example, perhaps because they have become uncompetitive, will put downward pressure on the pound (which is no longer needed in such quantities in order to purchase UK goods). If the exchange rate is flexible or **floating**, then the value of the pound will go down, but if the exchange rate is fixed then this cannot happen and the government must take action to preserve the fixed rate.

In Figure 95.1, the reduced demand for pounds reduces the exchange rate from P to P_1. In Figure 95.2 the government must reduce the supply of pounds onto the **foreign exchange market** (by buying them with **foreign currency reserves**) in order to preserve the fixed value of the pound P, figures 95.1 and 95.2.

In the ERM, the value of a currency is almost fixed and there could be large fluctuations in official reserves of foreign currencies as a result. Even though all countries in the ERM agree to help each other to maintain the rate set for their currencies, if there is considerable downward pressure on the pound, UK domestic rates of interest may have to be raised to persuade foreign investors to buy pounds (in order to invest in the UK to get the higher interest rates). This can lead to deflation of the economy and unemployment.

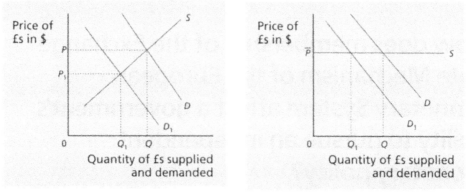

Figure 95.1 Floating exchange rate   Figure 95.2 Fixed exchange rate

An important argument against the ERM (and eventual **monetary union**) is that a government could not try to combat unemployment by allowing its currency to depreciate in the hope of raising demand for exports. Instead, wages and prices would have to fall to make exports more competitive, but this has implications for standards of living.

Conclusion

Membership of the ERM (and eventual monetary union) means that there must be harmonization of the economic policies of EC countries. In particular, inflation rates and public sector borrowing must be in line with other member states and this severely restricts the ability of an individual government to manage its own economy.

Further reading

→ Beardshaw, *chapter 40*
→ Lipsey and Chrystal, *pp. 761–2*
→ Parkin *et al.*, *chapter 36*

Economic growth

Examine the policies which a government might employ if it wishes to raise the rate of economic growth.

Introduction

Economic growth is an increase in an economy's level of **real output** over time. By specifying real output the effects of inflation are removed in order to find **real GNP**. Genuine economic growth also involves increased real **output per head** of population, or a rise in real GNP per capita.

Main arguments or theories

One of the most important determinants of economic growth is **investment**. A country which adds more to its capital stock year after year than other countries, should have a higher growth rate in the long term. The UK has a poor post-war investment record and this is at least partially responsible for low rates of economic growth relative to comparable developed countries. Policies to encourage investment could include tax concessions, longer patents, the use of long-term government contracts, and greater overall economic stability.

Since **saving** levels influence investment levels it may also make sense for governments to encourage savings. Japan's savings rate has been very high since 1960, while that of the UK and USA has been low. A problem here is that high **interest rates** to encourage saving would damage investment (because much investment is made using borrowed money, and high interest rates lead to reduced demand). So alternative encouragements to saving, such as **tax incentives**, must be used.

Appropriate **infrastructure** provided by government, such as roads, ports, airports, and railways, will enable firms to expand and facilitate economic growth. **Public sector investment** itself can be a big contributor to growth.

Policies to promote **exports** will increase production and therefore contribute to economic growth. For the UK this could be particularly important because there is evidence to suggest that the poor economic growth rates experienced since 1945 have been linked to weakness in the **balance of payments**. Every **growth spurt** involves an increase in imports and, as incomes increase, a fall in exports as domestic consumption rises. The consequent highly cyclical nature of the UK economy is not conducive to sustained investment or savings or economic growth.

Economic Growth   239

Policies such as tax advantages to exporters, trade fairs, and export drives could help to ensure consistent long-term growth.

The quality of the labour force in terms of its **education** or **skill level** is a very important determinant of growth. A highly skilled worker contributes far more to the economy than a manual worker—his **productivity** is higher. Since national output equals national income and a graduate's income is on average in the UK at least 150 per cent of that of a non-graduate, educating more people to degree level will increase GNP. There is much evidence to suggest that investment in improving the quality of the labour force in terms of its education and health is the single most effective determinant of economic growth. In the UK in the past decade numbers entering higher education have increased significantly to 30 per cent of the relevant age range, which approaches Japanese and German levels.

Conclusion

Governments must encourage savings, investment, and exports in order to increase the rate of economic growth. In the UK policies to achieve stability rather than a boom-and-bust economy would encourage investment. Over the longer term, investment in education and training is likely to be the most important influence on growth.

Further reading

→ Beardshaw, *chapter 45*
→ Lipsey and Chrystal, *chapter 33*
→ Parkin *et al.*, *chapter 26*

Discuss the view that the costs of economic growth outweigh the benefits.

Introduction

Economic growth is one of the main aims of government policy. This is because it can lead to higher **living standards** for the general population. With growth, people can enjoy more goods, more leisure, more education, and so on. Since the 1970s, however, some economists have argued that the costs of economic growth such as **pollution** are greater than the benefits.

Main arguments or theories

Living standards are undoubtedly increased by economic growth. Even at modest growth rates, such as those achieved in the UK since 1945, living standards in money terms can be expected to double within a generation. Moreover, growth can help to alleviate poverty since it is easier to reduce income inequalities without having to make anyone worse off. New products are invented, more effective sanitation and curative and preventive medicine are made possible by growth, and leisure time can be increased.

In the developed world sustained growth has provided travel, universal literacy, mass-produced goods, labour-saving consumer durables, and not least, increased life expectancy. It is no wonder that the less-developed and developing economies are pursuing policies aimed at rapid economic growth.

World economic collapse was predicted in 1972 by Meadows *et al.* in *The Limits to Growth*. Their view was that at current rates of growth the world would use up and exhaust supplies of vital finite resources, such as oil, gas, copper, iron, and zinc, within a relatively short period of time. Improved technology and new discoveries of resources have offset their rather **Malthusian** prediction, but they could still be proved correct in the future.

By 1992, at the Rio de Janeiro conference on the environment, attention had turned away from depletion issues and towards those of pollution.

Growth creates pollution, a **negative externality** which causes potentially devastating problems such as global warming, acid rain, and desertification. In underdeveloped countries it is often accompanied by deforestation and rapid population growth, while in the developed world it may lead to stressful lifestyles, traffic congestion, and the use of uncertain technologies such as genetic engineering and nuclear power generation.

Conclusion

Recent evidence from the World Bank suggests that the OECD countries (which are developed industrial nations) have reduced their pollution levels as their GNP has risen by using regulation and incentives. The suggestion is that economic growth can continue with the right policies to restrict damage to the environment. This is known as **sustainable development**.

Further reading

→ Beardshaw, *chapter 46*
→ Lipsey and Chrystal, *chapter 33*
→ Parkin *et al.*, *chapter 26*

Discuss the recent economic growth performance of the UK.

Economic growth is an increase in a country's productive capacity which is shown by a continuous rise in **real national income** over a period of years. This is normally identified by rising **real GNP per capita**.

Since 1945 the UK has had an average annual growth rate of about 2.5 per cent, which is significantly less than some late-developing countries such as Japan but also slightly less than comparable developed countries such as Germany, the United States, and France. Various reasons have been suggested for this **'British disease'**, some of which are discussed here.

Main arguments and theories

Although income per head has grown in the UK, it has grown at a slower rate than in other major developed nations. The UK's share of world manufacturing has fallen, along with relative **productivity** (output per worker). For a brief period in the mid-1980s UK growth exceeded that of most of our trading partners. This was partly because of the success of government **supply-side policies**, but also because of the boost to the economy provided by North Sea oil. Since then growth rates, although very variable, have fallen back to the (disappointing) long-term trend of about 2.5 per cent.

Government policy may be a reason for this, with the **'stop–go' policies** of the 1950s and 1960s being continued in a boom-and-slump repetition in the 1980s and 1990s, which is partly because of preoccupation with the inflation rate and **monetary policy** and possibly linked to an electoral cycle whereby the government stimulates the economy before an election in search of the 'feel-good factor'.

Other explanations of the UK's relatively poor growth performance include: the problems caused by **trade unions**, poor **management**, an **outflow of capital** to other countries, a poor education and training system, poor-quality **investment** and short-term policy for investment.

The UK has a relatively poor investment record (gross domestic fixed capital formation as a percentage of GDP) compared with Germany, France, and Italy from 1960 to 1990. The UK annual figure of approximately 18 per cent is similar to that of the USA and annual growth rates are also similar. This suggests that the key to economic growth for a developed economy such as the UK is to invest a significant proportion of GDP.

Conclusion

The UK has not performed as well as other industrialized countries in terms of rates of growth in the years 1945–96. The annual average growth rate of approximately 2.5 per cent is disappointing but because of its great variability and the cycle of boom and bust which has developed, the record is more disappointing still. With each recession a further part of the **manufacturing base** of the economy is lost, and this process of **deindustrialization** is unlikely to be halted without a major improvement in the quantity and quality of UK investment.

Further reading

→ Artis, *chapter 1*

→ Beardshaw, *chapter 45*

→ Parkin *et al.*, *chapter 26*

Macroeconomic policy

Identify and explain the principal macroeconomic policy objectives.

Introduction

The government of the UK has allowed one particular policy objective to dominate its actions since the 1970s: the control of **inflation**. On the grounds that this must be done before any other objective, such as a reduction in unemployment, can be achieved, successive governments have used **fiscal** and **monetary policies** to curb inflation.

Main arguments or theories

There are essentially four principal objectives of macroeconomic policy:

- a **stable level of prices** or low inflation
- **full employment**
- a satisfactory **growth of output**
- a satisfactory **balance of payments** and exchange rate

A fifth objective has been out of favour in recent times—that of redistributing income to achieve greater equity.

Low inflation is believed to be a prerequisite for achievement of any other objective, because with high rates of inflation there will be instability and uncertainty in the economy, which will adversely affect investment, savings, output plans, wages, and efficiency. Recent rises in the rate of inflation, particularly in the early 1980s and early 1990s, have been followed by a rise in the **rate of interest** to slow down the economy. The resulting fall in output, employment, and incomes succeeded in reducing the inflation rate.

Full employment (or very low unemployment of only around 2 per cent) was achieved in the UK between 1945 and 1970. Any increase in unemployment would be met by an increase in aggregate demand, which increased output, employment, and incomes. This became much more difficult after 1970 because of the rise in the underlying rate of inflation, which would be made worse by increased demand.

Economic growth in the UK has followed a long-term trend of approximately 2.5 per cent of GDP per annum although there is considerable variation in the short term. Economic growth improves material living standards and for this reason all governments wish to increase it. At times, however, it has to take second place as a policy objective to either the balance of payments (as with 1950s and 1960s **'stop–go' policy**) or inflation (as in the early 1980s and 1990s).

The balance of payments has been a problem for Britain for decades, as can be seen by the consistent decline in the value of the pound (**exchange rate**) against other major currencies. Any prolonged period of economic growth seems to 'suck in' imports in the form of raw materials and consumer goods (because workers have higher incomes). This constraint of the weakness of the balance of payments may be an important reason for the relatively weak growth performance of the UK economy.

Conclusion

Very often, the economic policy objectives of government can conflict and there may be a **trade-off** between them. For example, it may be difficult to achieve economic growth without an increase in the rate of inflation, or reduced inflation without higher unemployment, or an improvement in the balance of payments without a fall in output and employment.

Further reading

→ Artis, *chapter 5*
→ Beardshaw, *chapters 41–5*
→ Lipsey and Chrystal, *chapter 44*
→ Parkin *et al.*, *chapter 34*

To what extent is it true that pursuit of one macroeconomic policy objective involves a trade-off in terms of the worsening of a different macroeconomic target?

Introduction

In the UK different phases of economic history can often be associated with a particular economic problem. The 1920s and 1930s were beset by high **unemployment**, while the post-war period was characterized by successive **balance of payments** crises, which occurred whenever the **economic growth rate** increased. Since 1970, however, the dominant economic problem, and the one towards which economic policy has been directed, has been **inflation**.

Main arguments or theories

The four major macroeconomic aims of government are: **full employment** (or low unemployment), a satisfactory balance of payments position, sustainable economic growth, and **stable prices** (or low inflation). In attempting to improve any one of these, the policies which the government use may have adverse effects in another area. Hence they may have to 'trade off' an improvement in one economic variable such as unemployment with a worsening of another, such as inflation.

One such trade-off is that between the balance of payments and economic growth. During the 1950s and 1960s any improvement in the economic growth rate of the UK tended to be accompanied by a worsening of the balance of payments as the increased output necessitated greater imports of raw materials and higher incomes led to more spending on imports by consumers. This led to what became known as **'stop–go' policy** as the government had to stop economic growth periodically in order to improve the trade deficit. This would appear to be an inherent weakness of the UK economy which continues because of our dependence on imported raw materials.

Another trade-off is that between economic growth and inflation. As output, employment, and incomes increase with the rate of economic growth, so do inflationary pressures, and the economy may 'overheat' with both **cost-push** (from the labour market) and **demand-pull** (because of higher spending) **inflation** gathering momentum. Such a situation occurred in Britain in the late 1980s and remedial action, in the form of a drastic slowdown in the rate of economic growth, was necessary to bring the rate of inflation down from 10 per cent, which it reached in 1990.

The policy trade-off which has received the most attention is that between unemployment and inflation. The **Phillips Curve** suggests such a trade-off and in the past governments have believed that a low level of unemployment would lead to a high level of inflation. The apparent breakdown of this relationship in the 1970s (which was characterized by *both* high inflation and high unemployment) led to increasingly sophisticated interpretations of the Phillips Curve, but there still appears to be significant negative correlation between the two variables.

Conclusion

Employment and economic growth will be improved by expansionary economic policies, while the inflation rate and the UK balance of payments seem to improve with contractionary economic policies. Clearly then there will be a conflict if any one of these aims is targeted which will lead to a worsening of at least one of the others. It may be possible to avoid this 'trade-off' if a stable price level precedes a period of sustainable economic growth, and it is towards this that current government policy is directed.

Further reading

→ Artis, *chapter 5*
→ Beardshaw, *chapter 41*
→ Lipsey and Chrystal, *chapter 44*
→ Parkin *et al.*, *chapter 34*

List of Abbreviations and Symbols

AC	average cost	**MRPL**	marginal revenue product of labour
AD	aggregate demand		
AFC	average fixed cost	*MS*	money supply
APC	average propensity to consume	*MSC*	marginal social cost
AR	average revenue	*MU*	marginal utility
ARP	average revenue product	**NAIRU**	non-accelerating inflation rate of unemployment
AS	aggregate supply		
ATC	average total cost	**NNP**	net national product
AVC	average variable cost	*NPV*	net present value
C	consumption	*NR*	non-reaction curve
CAP	Common Agricultural Policy	**OECD**	Organization for Economic Co-operation and Development
CBA	cost-benefit analysis		
D	demand	**OFGAS**	Office of the Gas Regulator
DL	demand for labour	**OFT**	Office of Fair Trading
ERM	Exchange Rate Mechanism	**OFTEL**	Office of the Telecom-munications Regulator
EU	European Union		
f	is a function of	**OFWAT**	Office of the Water Regulator
FC	fixed cost	**OPEC**	Organisation of Petroleum Exporting Countries
G	government expenditure		
GATT	General Agreement on Trade and Tariffs	*P*	price
		$P_1 \ldots {}_n$	prices of other goods (affecting demand)
GDP	gross domestic product		
GNP	gross national product	$P_{f1} \ldots {}_n$	prices of factors of production (affecting supply)
i	interest rate		
I	investment	*PC*	potential competition price
K	multiplier	*PED*	price elasticity of demand
L	loanable funds	*PMC*	private marginal cost
LRAC	long-run average cost	**PPC**	production possibilities curve
M	imports	**PSBR**	Public Sector Borrowing Requirement
MB	marginal benefits		
MC	marginal cost	*Q*	quantity
MD	money demand	*QD*	quantity demanded
MEC	marginal efficiency of capital	*QS*	quantity supplied
		Rc	reaction curve
MEI	marginal efficiency of invest-ment	*R/I*	rate of interest
		RPC	Restrictive Practices Court
MMC	Monopolies and Mergers Commission	**RPI**	Retail Prices Index
		S	supply
MPC	marginal propensity to consume	*SA*	saving
		SMB	social marginal benefit
MPrC	marginal private cost	**SMC**	social marginal cost
MR	marginal revenue	**SRAC**	short-run average cost
MRP	marginal revenue product	*t*	tastes (affecting demand)

TC	total cost	**WTO**	World Trade Organization
T_y	technology (affecting supply)	*X*	exports
TPI	Taxes and Prices Index	*Y*	income
TR	total revenue	Y_E	equilibrium level of national income
TU	total utility		
U	utility	Y_F	full-employment level of national output
UK	United Kingdom		
USSR	Union of Soviet Socialist Republics (former Soviet Union)	*YED*	income elasticity of demand
		Δ	change (or a change in)
		∞	infinity
V	volume of traffic	$<$	less than
VAT	Value Added Tax	$>$	greater than
W	wage rate		

abnormal profit 42, 68
absolute advantage 223, 224
Absolute Income Hypothesis 137, 139
accelerator principle 154, 156, 163, 164–6, 168
accelerator theory *see* accelerator principle
administrative economies 63
advertising 35
aggregate demand 127, 128, 149, 155, 156–8, 169, 170, 182, 193, 194, 196, 211, 213, 214, 216, 247
aggregate expenditure 193
aggregate supply 105, 127, 128, 211, 213, 214
agriculture 37, 129
allocation of resources 48
allocative inefficiency 117
assumptions 11, 67
automatic stabilisers 195
autonomous consumption 137
autonomous investment 153
average cost (AC) 59, 63, 70
average fixed cost (AFC) 61
average propensity to consume 140
average revenue (AR) 68, 73
average total cost (ATC) 61
average variable cost (AVC) 61, 62

balanced budget multiplier 161, 162
balance of payments 201, 225, 226, 233, 234, 239, 247–50
Bank of England 171, 172, 179–82, 185, 196, 233
barriers to entry 75, 76, 77, 79, 81, 83, 87
base rates 171
beef 19
black economy 134
black market 16, 24, 25
Black Wednesday 182, 235
bonds 185
boom 20, 195, 246
brewing 60
Bristol 115
British Coal 107
'British disease' 243
British Gas 105, 108, 117
British Rail 117
British Steel 107
British Telecom 105, 117
broad money 175

budget 31, 32, 161, 162, 195, 196
budget deficit 191, 195
bureaucracy 20
business cycle 163, 164, 166, 167
business expectations 154

capital consumption 133, 153
capital gains tax 48
capital goods 13
capitalist system 167
capital market 185, 186
capital-to-output ratio 156, 164, 166
cartel 89
cash ratio 181
ceiling price 23, 25
certificates of deposit 175, 177
ceteris paribus 11
Chancellor of the Exchequer 195
Channel Tunnel 97
choices 17
cigarettes 31
circular flow in income 129, 131, 140, 147, 165, 195
clearing banks 179, 181
closed shop 81
collective bargaining 81
collective ownership 15
collusion 77, 78, 89
command economy 15
commercial banks 185, 191
commercial economies 63
Common Agricultural Policy (CAP) 43, 229
Common External Tariff 229, 230
common market 229
common property resource 99
comparative advantage 223, 229
competition 76, 117
competition policy 83
concentration of ownership 119
concentration ratio 60
conspicuous consumption 138
construction 109, 129
consumer durables 127, 141
consumer expenditure deflator (CED) 199
consumer goods 141, 155
consumer spending 137, 141, 147, 155, 156, 194
consumers' surplus 85, 86, 88, 97
consumption 141, 145, 149, 155, 164, 193

consumption function 137
copyright 79
Corporation Tax 49
cost–benefit analysis 14, 95, 96, 97, 98
cost of living 199, 200
cost per unit of output 59
cost–push inflation 208, 226, 249
coursework 1
craft unions 81
credit 183
credit creation 175, 181
crowding-out effect 190, 192, 194, 195
current account 225, 226
customs union 229
cyclical instability 37
cyclical unemployment 211

deficit financing 191
deflation 204, 235
deflationary gap 157, 158, 169, 170, 193, 194
deflationary policy 233
deforestation 241
deindustrialization 244
demand 19, 20, 39
demand curve 97
demand-deficient unemployment 211
demand function 29
demand management 168, 205, 207
demand pull inflation 127, 203, 249
demerit good 31
depreciation 134, 153, 225
depressed areas 115
depression 170
deregulation 39, 105, 117, 216
derived demand 45, 51
devaluation 225, 226
differentiated products 73
direct intervention 193
direct taxation 105, 189
discount houses 171, 185
discounting 95
discount rate 95, 97
discount stores 119
disincentives 194
disintermediation 176
disposable income 137, 145, 149, 157
dissaving 137
division of labour 57, 58
double-counting 129
dumping 44

economic activity 163, 167, 168, 177, 191, 203
economic growth 16, 28, 106, 146, 148, 156, 201, 204, 208, 217, 226, 239–44, 247, 249, 250
economic models 11
economic rent 47, 48
economics dictionary 3
economies of scale 59, 71, 83, 87, 230
economies of scope 63
education 20, 129, 141, 206, 216, 240, 243
education vouchers 113
elastic demand 28, 88
elasticity 27, 38
electoral cycle 163, 168, 243
empirical evidence 12, 137, 140, 159, 190, 207, 215
employment 50, 163, 201, 204, 248, 250
engineering 59
enterprise 49
entrepreneurial spirit 15
entrepreneurs 15
entrepreneurship 109, 110
environmental consequences 44, 241, 242
Equal Pay Act 52, 53
equilibrium national income 131
equilibrium price 29, 30, 39
equities 185
European Monetary System 235, 236
European Union 117, 229, 230, 235, 236
excess capacity 35, 69, 127
excess demand 25, 194
excess supply 45
exchange control 229
exchange rate 178, 225–8, 233–6, 247, 248
Exchange Rate Mechanism (ERM) 177, 178, 182, 225, 233, 236
exchequer 121, 217
excise duty 31
expectations 39, 145, 154, 157
expenditure–income diagram 171
exports 127, 155, 193, 201, 225–8, 233–6, 239, 240
external cost 111
externalities 14, 18, 93, 94, 95, 96, 99

factor cost 95
factor of production 30, 47, 79
factor payments 131
Fair Trading Act (1973) 117
farm incomes 43
'feel good factor' 243

financial economies 63
financial institutions 147
financial markets 39
Financial Times 4
fiscal policy 169, 170, 191, 193, 194, 196,
    214, 216, 247
fixed costs 61
fixed exchange rates 225, 233–5
floating exchange rates 225, 233, 235
floor price 24, 45
foreign currency reserves 235
foreign exchange market 235
freedom of entry 75
free enterprise economy 16, 50
free good 100
free market system 61, 107
free trade 223
frictional unemployment 211, 212
Friedman, M. 137, 145
full employment 127, 132, 169, 170, 201,
    207, 211, 213, 217, 247, 249
full employment level of output 157, 193,
    214

Galbraith, J. K. 84
game theory 78, 90
General Agreement on Tariffs and Trade
    (GATT) 224, 229
geographical mobility 219, 220
gilts 181, 185
glossary of terms 3
GNP deflator 134
government intervention 15
government policy 243
government spending 131, 140, 191, 193,
    194, 195
gross domestic product 15, 16, 129, 130, 137,
    153, 155, 166, 196, 211, 213, 243, 244,
    247
gross investment 153
gross national product 133, 190, 217, 218,
    239, 242

hairdressing 63
health 20, 129
Hicks–Kaldor Criterion 97
homogeneous products 67
household formation 39
house prices 115, 116, 219, 220
housing 39, 141, 219
human capital 141, 142, 217

imperfect competition 35, 69, 70, 73, 75
imports 155, 193, 201, 223, 225, 226–9, 233,
    234, 239, 248
incentives 189, 216
income 39, 50, 101, 137, 138, 139, 140, 163
income distribution 133, 247
income effect 190
income elasticity of demand 27, 28
income tax 105
indirect taxes 28, 105, 155
indivisibilities 79
induced investment 153
industrial unions 81
inelastic demand 27, 31, 37, 86, 89
inelastic supply 37, 39
infant industries 224
inferior goods 28
inflation 16, 134, 145, 161, 168, 177, 178–80,
    182, 191, 192, 194, 196, 197, 199,
    201–8, 214–16, 236, 247–50
inflationary gap 158, 169, 170, 194
inflationary spiral 204
infrastructure 239
inheritance tax 101
injection 131, 132, 148, 155, 165
insurance companies 185
interbank market 185
interdependent actions (of firms) 77
interest 171
interest-bearing security 157
interest rate 127, 145, 149, 150, 153, 157, 164,
    168, 171, 172, 175, 177, 178, 180–2, 183,
    192, 201, 202, 204, 233–5, 239, 247
International Stock Exchange 186
international trade 223, 224
intervention 23
intervention buying 43
inventories 141, 163
inventory cycle 167
investment 16, 127, 131, 140, 141, 145,
    147–58, 164, 166, 168, 193, 195, 201,
    202, 234, 239, 240, 243, 246
investment trusts 185
invisible hand 17, 19
inward investment 115, 116
iron and steel 60

J-curve effect 225

Keynes, John Maynard 3, 131, 137, 139, 145,
    149, 153, 157, 168, 170, 183, 191, 213, 216

kinked demand curve 77
Kondratieff cycle 167
Kuznets cycle 167

Laffer Curve 189, 190
laissez-faire 23, 31
Lamont, Norman 216
last-resort lending 171, 179
leakage 131
least-cost output 69
lender of last resort *see* last-resort lending
Life-Cycle Hypothesis 138, 145
liquid assets 183, 191
liquid money 180
liquidity 175
liquidity preference 183, 184
liquidity ratio 182
living standards 16, 133, 199, 217, 227, 236,
    241, 247
loanable funds 158
Loanable Funds Theory 149
Lorenz curve 101
Luddites 57
lump sum tax 31

M_0 (money) 175, 177
M_1 (money) 175, 177, 182
M_2 (money) 175
M_3 (money) 175, 177, 182
M_4 (money) 175
M1 motorway 95, 96
macro-economic policy 166, 247, 249
Malthus, Thomas 241
management 243
manufactured goods 37, 38
manufacturing 59, 63, 109
manufacturing base 244
marginal benefits 100
marginal efficiency of capital (MEC) 150,
    153
marginal efficiency of investment, *see* mar-
    ginal efficiency of capital
marginal physical product 51
marginal private costs 100, 111
marginal product 101
marginal propensity to consume 139, 155,
    161, 163, 165
marginal rate of tax 189, 191
marginal revenue product (MRP) 45, 51, 53
marginal social costs 100, 111
market failure 18, 100

market forces 15, 17
market imperfections 14
market price 19
market share 63, 119
market structure 73
Marshall–Lerner Condition 225
mass production 57
maximum price 23
Meadows Report 241
medium of exchange 175, 176, 181, 183
medium term financial strategy 177, 178
merchant banks 185
merger 83
merit bads 31
merit goods 18, 113, 114
microeconomic policies 105
Middlesborough 115
mineral products 37
minimum wage 23, 25, 26, 45
mobility of labour 217
Modigliani, Ando, and Brumberg 138, 145
monetarism 177, 178
monetarists 191, 207, 211, 215
monetary aggregates 175
monetary base control 180
monetary policy 169, 170, 172, 17, 179, 193,
    194, 214, 216, 243, 247
monetary squeeze 208
monetary targets 177, 182
monetary union 229, 236
money markets 171, 185, 186
money multiplier 179, 181
money supply 163, 171, 172, 175, 177, 179,
    181, 182, 191
Monopolies and Mergers Commission 64,
    82, 83, 117
monopolistic competition 73
monopoly 20, 42, 63, 75, 79, 83, 86, 87, 95,
    108, 117
monopsony 46
mortgage rate 39
motor cars 29, 60, 77
multiple stores 119
multiplier 140, 155, 161, 163–6, 168, 170, 189

narrow money 175
national debt 191, 196
national expenditure 129
national income 129, 131, 140, 154–6, 160,
    161, 165, 166, 169, 170, 189, 190, 193,
    195, 214

national income accounts 199
national output 129
nationalization 107
nationalized industry 83
natural barriers 75
natural monopoly 83, 84, 118
natural rate of unemployment 106, 205,
    206, 211, 214, 215
near-money 175
negative externality 97, 111, 241
neo-classical economics 39, 213
net exports 193
net investment 153
net national product 133
net present value 95
newspaper sources 3
niche market 59
non-accelerating inflation rate of unemploy-
    ment (NAIRU) 208, 211, 215
non-excludability 111, 112
non-intervention 23
non-price competition 35
non-rival 111
normal profit 41, 49, 68
North American Free Trade Area (NAFTA)
    229
North Sea Oil 243
North Sea Oil Royalties 48, 116
North–South divide 115, 116

occupational mobility 219, 220
OECD 242
Office of Fair Trading 117
OFGAS 108
OFTEL 108, 118
OFWAT 108, 118
oligopoly 75, 89
OPEC 90, 203
open access 99
open market operations 171, 179, 181, 182
opportunity cost 13, 41, 95, 142, 150, 153,
    183, 217
opportunity cost of capital 95
optimum technical output 69, 70
over-exploitation 99
over-fishing 93

paradox of thrift 147
Pareto criterion 97
patents 79, 80, 239
pension funds 185

perfect competition 11, 42, 67, 69, 70, 75
Permanent Income Hypothesis 137, 145
petrol 28
Phillips, A. W. 215, 216
Phillips Curve 201, 205, 207, 208, 212, 250
physical capital 142
planned economy 19
plough-back 50
polluter pays principle 93
pollution 18, 93, 99, 100, 241, 242
pollution permits 100
positive externality 113, 114
potential Pareto improvement 97
precautionary motive 145, 183
present value 95, 97
price discrimination 85, 86
price elasticity of demand 27, 31, 32
price index 199
price level 127
price mechanism 17
price rigidity 89
prices 15
price-taker 67
price war 78, 89
primary products 37, 38
private costs 4, 93, 94, 95
private enterprize 105
private marginal cost *see* marginal private
    cost
private sector 107, 161, 179, 189, 191
privatization 83, 84, 105, 107, 108, 117, 121,
    122, 191, 206, 216
product differentiation 79
production goods 155
production possibilities curve 13
productivity 51, 57, 105, 106, 189, 213, 240,
    243
profit 15, 20, 41, 49, 50, 61, 63, 89
profit maximization 69
Progressive taxes 101, 113, 189
property rights 99
protectionism 224, 229
PSL_2 (money) 177
public finance 217
public goods 18, 111, 113
public interest 63, 64, 83, 108, 117
public ownership 83
public sector 15, 95, 97, 107, 185, 236
public sector borrowing requirement
    (PSBR) 105, 121, 161, 178, 181, 182, 185,
    191, 192, 195, 196

public sector investment 190, 239
public spending 217
pure monopoly 81

Quantity Theory of Money 203
quasi-money 175
quasi-rents 42
quotas 229
quotations 3

rate of interest *see* interest rate
rational expectations 145
rationing 25
real GNP 239, 243
real interest rate 145, 149, 154
real output 239
recession 114, 116, 168, 195, 204, 208, 212,
    216, 217, 234
recovery 168, 234
redistribution of income 113
regional policy 115
regulation 83, 84
Rents Acts 24, 26
research and development 80, 87
reserve assets 179
reserve assets ratio 181
reserve ratio 179
resources 13, 17
re-spending effect 140, 161, 166
restrictive practices 79, 83, 84, 87, 105, 117,
    118
retail deposits 175
Retail Prices Index (RPI) 199, 200
retailing 119, 120
revenue 28, 61, 62
revision 1
Ricardo, David 223, 224
risk 41, 50
road pricing 111
Robinson, Joan 11
Roskill Commission 97

Saudi Arabia 90
saving 131, 132, 145–50, 157, 158, 201, 239,
    240
savings function 147
savings gap 157
savings ratio 146
Say, J. B. 105
Say's Law 149, 157, 213
seasonally adjusted 211

seasonal unemployment 211
Schumpeter, Joseph 87
Secretary of State for Trade and Industry
    117
securities 185
self-consumed produce 134
self-employment 109
sellers preferences 24
service sector 59, 109, 115
'set aside' 44
Sex Discrimination Act 53
shadow prices 95, 96, 97
share ownership 107, 121
shift in demand 37
sight deposits 175, 177
skill shortages 217, 219
skills mismatch 211
Singapore 112
slump 20
Smith, Adam 17, 57
social benefits 18, 97
social costs 4, 93, 94, 95, 97
social marginal benefit 93
social marginal cost *see* marginal social cost
social opportunity costs 14
social rate of time preference 95
social science 11
Soviet Union 19
special deposits 179, 181, 182
specialization 57, 58, 71, 223
speculative motive 183
spillover effects 18, 93
stable prices 201, 247, 249
stagflation 206
standard of living *see* living standards
state monopolies 121
Sterling M$_3$ 177
stocks 185
stop–go policies 243, 248, 249
structural change 219
structural unemployment 211, 212
structure–conduct–performance models
    67, 75
style 3
subcontracting 71
subheadings 5
subsidies 95
subsistence level 57
substitute 29, 31, 79
substitution effect 190
supernormal profit 41, 42, 48, 68, 76, 79

supply 39
supply function 29
supply shocks 37, 43, 203
supply side policy 105, 109, 189, 190, 206,
    214, 216, 243
sustainable development 242

take over 121
tariffs 229
tax incentives 239
taxes 95, 131, 161, 194, 195, 217
Taxes and Prices Index (TPI) 199
technical economies 63
technological unemployment 57, 211
temporary monopoly 79
terms of trade 227, 228
terms of trade index 227
theory of the firm 67
time deposits 175, 177
tobacco 28, 31
trade 57, 223, 224
trade barriers 229
trade cycle 154, 166–8
trade diversion 229
trade fairs 240
trade-offs 201, 248–50
trade restriction 224
trade surpluses 227
trades unions 52, 81, 82, 206, 216, 219, 243
trading blocs 229
traffic congestion 93
tragedy of the commons 99
transactions motive 183

transfer earnings 47
transfer payments 101
Treasury Bills 175, 179, 181, 191

uncertainty 78, 90, 201, 202
unemployment 24, 44, 105, 115, 131, 148,
    193, 195, 205–14, 216–20, 230, 235,
    236, 247–50
unemployment benefit 206, 217, 224
unit trusts 185
unrecorded transactions 134
USSR 16
utilities 107, 121

value added 129, 130
Value Added Tax 31
value judgement 113
velocity of circulation 203
voluntary unemployment 216

waiting lists 25
wants 141
warehouse price clubs 119
wealth 101, 116, 127, 145
Wealth of Nations 17
welfare 88, 105, 113, 134
welfare loss 117
withdrawal 131, 132, 147, 155
working population 109
World Bank 242
World Trade Organization (WTO) 224

X-efficient 83

Lightning Source UK Ltd.
Milton Keynes UK
UKHW031133130320
360219UK00014B/417